GERALD T. SHEPPARD

is Associate Professor of Old Testament Literature and Exegesis in Emmanuel College of Victoria University and the Toronto School of Theology in the University of Toronto. Raised in the Assemblies of God (pentecostal) churches, he attended Fuller Theological Seminary, then pursued further study at Yale Divinity School and Yale University, leading to a doctorate in Old Testament studies. Prior to his current, fifth year of teaching at Emmanuel, Sheppard taught nine years at Union Theological Seminary in New York City. There he served on the executive steering committee of the Faith and Order Movement of the National Council of Christian Churches and he worked in a wide variety of churches. He is well-known for his publications on ecumenical issues regarding contemporary biblical interpretation. As an Old Testament scholar, he has earned an international reputation, especially for his work on prophetic and wisdom literature. His commentary on Isaiah 1-39 appeared recently in the *Harper's Bible Commentary* (1988). He has previously published a monograph on wisdom literature, *Wisdom as a Hermeneutical Construct*, and numerous articles in journals, books, encyclopedias and dictionaries. This year he edited essays (including his own) in connection with two separate reprints: the Geneva New Testament of 1602 and William Perkin's commentary on Galatians of 1611. The Geneva New Testament with its extensive marginal notes was the first widely accepted Protestant "preachers" Bible which predominated for nearly a century prior to the popularity of the so-called King James Version. These classic seventeenth-century books and the forthcoming volumes in the series, including commentaries on the Old Testament, have excited interest among students of both English literature and of the history of biblical interpretation and theology.

The
FUTURE
of the
BIBLE

Beyond Liberalism and Literalism

The

FUTURE
of the
BIBLE

Beyond Liberalism and Literalism

GERALD T. SHEPPARD

THE UNITED CHURCH PUBLISHING HOUSE
1990

Copyright © 1990 The United Church Publishing House,
The United Church of Canada
ISBN - 0-919000-60-6

Publisher: R. L. Naylor
Editor-in-Chief: Peter Gordon White
Editorial Assistant: Elizabeth Phinney
Book Design: Graphics & Print Production
Printing: Thistle Printing Limited

Canadian Cataloguing in Publication Data

Sheppard, Gerald T., 1946-
    The future of the Bible

Includes bibliographical references.
ISBN 0-919000-60-6

1. Bible - Criticism, interpretation, etc.
2. Bible. O.T. Psalms - Criticism, interpretation,
etc. 3. Wisdom literature - Criticism,
interpretation, etc. I. Title

BS511.2.S48 1990   220.6   C90-093231-7

890233

CONTENTS

III

SOLOMIC WISDOM LITERATURE: HOW SHOULD WE ANSWER THE RIDDLES OF THE QUEEN OF SHEBA?

Preface

This work grows out of public lectures that I was invited to deliver during Convocation Week, in May, 1989, at Emmanuel College, where I teach. Due to the complexity and wider implications of what I wanted to present, I soon realized that I could not simply publish those three lectures. In this book the topics of the lectures have been retained, though the content is developed for more extensively than the lecture setting could allow. I owe many thanks to the faculty and especially Principal Douglas Jay who gave me this challenging opportunity.

Among the limitations of what I offer here is my awareness that I am only beginning to understand some of the cultural, social, historical, and ecclesial dimensions of my new home in Canada. I have ventured some nascent interpretations of the Canadian situation, with considerable help from scholarly colleagues Phyllis Airhart and John Webster Grant, who will, I hope, not be embarassed by the paucity of what I could contribute. At the same time, my role as a teacher in Old Testament literature is betrayed by the minimal development here of New Testament implications. What is done here with the Old Testament already presumes its possibility in the light of the New and I have drawn direct connections here and there. Still, a fully adequate treatment of the same issues within the New Testament itself would need to go far beyond the limits of this study.

Principal Douglas C. Jay graciously read through the entire manuscript and offered many invaluable suggestions. Also, faculty colleague, the late David Newman, provided me with perceptive criticisms of the manuscript, as did doctoral students, Christine Gross and Susanne Abbuhl. Peter White, editor of The United Church Publishing House, had unusual patience, encouragement, and wisdom in the process of publishing this book. I want to thank, above all, my wife Anne, who has been a colleague and inspiration at every level of this project. Her insight and hard work made a primary contribution to the production of this study. I dedicate this book to her, as an unworthy token of my appreciation.

I

HOW TO READ A BOOK THAT SEEMS INTENT ON READING YOU

A. INTRODUCTION

The present controversies regarding human sexuality, ordination, and inclusive language within The United Church of Canada are exacerbated by conflicting views regarding how scripture should be read and interpreted. The two principal options for interpreting scripture are often presented as "liberalism" and "literalism." Admittedly, these labels favor the self-described "liberal" side of the debate. Few, if any, Christians march voluntarily under a "literalist" banner. Those accused of "literalism" by their opponents prefer to call themselves "conservative," "traditionalist," "neo-orthodox," "evangelical," or any number of other labels except "fundamentalist." Behind the choice between "liberalism" or "literalism" lies a significant history of disputes over the nature of the Bible and the role of modern historical criticism, with its own distinctly Canadian character. My thesis is that this older debate should not block us from recognizing presently an entirely fresh recovery of "the Bible as scripture" that is currently emerging around us. Moreover, this understanding of the Bible draws strong lines of continuity with the past history of biblical interpretation but recognizes the discontinuity implicit with the rise of modern historical criticism. Its insights ought to change in practical ways how we argue from the Bible about matters of faith and conduct in the church.

This book derives from extensively revised lectures given at Emmanuel College during convocation week in May, 1989. The first chapter will set out a general proposal; the other two on Psalms and wisdom literature offer some illustrations from biblical texts of what I am proposing. In this opening chapter, I will initially make a few *ad hoc* observations about the past debate over the Bible in Canada and in the United States, then sketch some of the changes in biblical studies since the 1960's that ought to cause us, in the present debate, to view the older choice between liberalism and literalism as both misleading and obsolete.

1. Past Battles Over the Bible

In a chapter in his *A Profusion of Spires*, John Webster Grant has eloquently described the "Strains in the Fabric" that accompanied the rise of modern historical criticism of the Bible in the last two decades of the nineteenth century here in Canada.[1] If we compare Grant's presentation of events in Canada with what happened in the same debate in the United States, we might say that what were "strains in the fabric" in Canada became a "rent garment" in the United States. While seminary faculties were polarized in Canada and some biblical scholars were dismissed from their teaching positions, the landscape of the United States seemed, by comparison, littered with vestiges of split denominations and seminaries as well as the sudden appearance of entirely new, dissenting seminaries and Bible colleges. The reasons for these differences pertain to a dense variety of distinctions between the two countries including social, religious, political, economic, and cultural factors. Historians, who know much more

1. John Webster Grant, *A Profusion of Spires: Religion in Nineteenth-Century Ontario* (Toronto: Ontario Historical Studies Series, 1988), pp. 204-220.

about these matters than I, have already helped us understand much about this period.[2] My point here is only to underscore that if the debate has seemed institutionally less volatile in Canada than in the United States, the appropriation and use of historical criticism has remained no less a problem.

At the outset, I want to look briefly into the social and religious history of Canada and the United States in order to call attention to a couple of key features. First, in Canada, we should remind ourselves of what the language of liberalism and literalism once came to signify. For purposes of recalling the popular terminology that survives from that period, we can look back to a novel by a prominent Presbyterian minister, Charles W. Gordon, who, as many of you know, wrote under the name of Ralph Connor. In Connor's romantic novel *The Arm of Gold* published in 1932, we find an optimistic scenario set in the late 1920's about a liberally educated minister in a typical rural parish. Pastor MacGregor of the town's major protestant church has a conversation about the Bible with a kind-hearted, local skeptic, Mr. Marriott, who sporadically attends the church when prodded by his daughter. One day Mr. Marriott playfully questions how the pastor can accept the Genesis stories as a scientifically accurate account of creation. Pastor MacGregor, stunned that Mr. Marriott presumes he is so naive, retorts, "Do you mean the Genesis story as *literal* scientific truth? Mr. Marriott, you insult my intelligence and my religion. No, I do not. The Genesis writing sets forth truth, deep, marvellous, eternal truth. But as a scientific statement of world origins? No!"[3] The pastor fears that he has failed to make himself clear on these points in his sermons, so that a man

---

2. See, besides Grant's *A Profusion of Spires*: Tom Sinclair-Faulkner, "Theory Divided from Practice: The Introduction of Historical Criticism into Canadian Protestant Seminaries," *Studies in Religion* 10 (1981) 231-43; Robert Handy, "Alternative Visions of a Christian Canada (1867-1925)," pp. 344-76, *A History of the Churches in the United States and Canada* (New York: Oxford University Press, 1979); and forthcoming by Phyllis Airhart, *Serving the Present Age: Revivalism, Progressivism, and the Methodist Tradition* [a revision of Chicago Ph.D. Diss., 1985].

3. Ralph Connor, *The Arm of Gold* (Toronto: McClelland & Stewart, Limited, 1932), p. 89.

as intelligent as Mr. Marriott might still attribute to him "a theory of Scriptural interpretation discarded more than a quarter of a century ago by every Biblical scholar of any importance, certainly in Britain and Canada."[4] MacGregor, subsequently, preaches a series on "the modern view of Biblical interpretation," showing, on the one hand, that the Bible itself "was made up of a great mass of fragments"[5] and, on the other, that it is "the message of God to man," telling us "what ... to do" and "how ... to get home to Him."[6] Some parishioners are unnerved because they fear that MacGregor's approach might threaten the truth of the actual words of the text. Conversely, when the skeptic, Mr. Marriott, hears the sermon he is relieved of his objections to the Bible and suddenly becomes more open to the pastor's exposition of a message of faith from scripture. This presentation in Connor's novel illustrates well an older distinction associated with a "liberal" rather than a "literal" interpretation of scripture. The former is attentive to historical criticism and receptive to the current scientific and historical consensus, the latter naively assumes that the truth of the Bible is a divinely revealed alternative to modern ideas of science and history. The former is informed by contemporary scholarship and knowledge, the latter is not.

We observe that the older use of the terms liberalism and literalism specifically pertained to the impact of historical criticism. The adequacy of these terms even in that period may be questioned, but at least they corresponded to a specific debate about the nature of the Bible with obvious theological significance. After that period, the appearance of neo-orthodoxy and progressive types of evangelicalism alone demonstrate that the older divisions radically shifted and substantially changed. Consequently, I find that the hermeneutical and theological implications of the labels "liberal" and "literalist"

4. Connor, p. 190.

5. Connor, p. 192, 220.

6. Connor, p. 202.

4

have become increasingly vague to the point that they now serve more clearly to label for political advantage and, in some cases, libel, certain groups within the church than to signify live options of insight into scripture, biblical preaching, commentary, or theology.

Another aspect of Connor's story indicates an awareness that the situation "certainly in Britain and Canada" differs from circumstances in the United States. Two American visitors who are friends of MacGregor comment after he preaches about historical criticism and the Bible:

> "What would happen to a minister who preached that sermon of his down in our country?" said the doctor. "What would our Fundamentalists do to him?"

> "They'd give him hell, I guess," said Daphne. "No, it wouldn't do. They'd crucify him, damn them."[7]

This awareness that Canadian "literalism" was not the same as that "damn" fundamentalism in the United States leads me to make a related observation about a more recent battle over the Bible in the United States.

When I started teaching at Union Theological Seminary in New York City, *Time Magazine* heralded that year — 1976 — as "The Year of the Evangelicals." It is ironic that 1976 also proved to be the same year self-declared, conservative "evangelical" seminaries in the United States exploded in a fiery conflict over who really qualifies to be called an "evangelical." Harold Lindsell's book, *The Battle for the Bible*, exemplified the vitriolic nature of this crisis in evangelical identity by naming names and accusing various colleges and seminaries, such as Fuller Theological Seminary, of "liberalism" or of seduction by liberalism's chastened offspring, "neo-orthodoxy." Lindsell and his colleagues drew the battleline at the choice

---

7. Connor, p. 208.

between either confessing the true "inerrancy" of the Bible or, in concession to modern liberalism, affirming merely the "infallibility of scripture in matters of faith and practice."[8] Those who supported "inerrancy," in Lindsell's argument, confirmed their evangelical credentials, while those who preferred the term "infallibility" betrayed a less than orthodox position. Entire books have been written over the subsequent years on each side of this conflict. Fuller Theological Seminary, for example, defended its position in support of infallibility, aided by Jack Rogers and Donald McKim's *The Authority and Interpretation of Scripture* (1979). John Woodbridge from Trinity Evangelical Divinity School marshalled support for inerrancy in his *Biblical Criticism: A Critique of the Rogers-McKim Proposal* (1982). Of course, at stake in this exchange was more than a nuanced expression in the doctrine of scripture, but also tangible political and economic benefits for those publicly identified as "evangelical," including financial support of colleges, seminaries, parachurch groups, magazines, and publishing houses thriving as "evangelical" voices in the religious marketplace.

Now, as someone raised a pentecostal, who began theological studies at the center of "neo-evangelicalism," Fuller Theological Seminary, and who pursued doctoral studies at Yale, a "liberal" university, I have had personal reasons for trying to make some sense of this "Battle for the Bible" among evangelicals within the United States. I became fascinated with how the ardent defenders of the Bible, on both sides of this internal evangelical dispute, sought to defend their positions. At the outset, should it not seem a little strange that the strongest affirmations both sides could offer amount to the choice between two double negatives, inerrancy and infallibility? In other words, one group has the courage to say that the Bible is "not

---

8. Harold Lindsell, *The Battle for the Bible* (Grand Rapids: Zondervan, 1976), pp. 13, 200-101. See, also, his *The Bible in the Balance* (Grand Rapids: Zondervan, 1979), pp. 12-15, 50-59. Cf. Gerald T. Sheppard, "Biblical Hermeneutics: The Academic Language of Evangelical Identity," *Union Seminary Quarterly Review* 32/2 (1977) 81-94.

not correct," while the other boldly proclaims it is "not not true in matters of faith and practice." Meanwhile, the enemy of both positions is supposed to be "liberalism" which does not read the Bible for errors, but, as the "liberal" pastor MacGregor in Canada once said, for its "truth, deep, marvellous, eternal truth." The ambiguity on all sides about what is an "error" and the agreement on the prevailing truth of scripture made me suspicious. In these evangelical disputes, I began to realize the term "inerrancy" functioned less theologically as an affirmation of scripture than politically as a password into the confidence of a particular socioeconomic consortium of believers with their own presses, denominational groups, and educational institutions.

You will not be surprised, then, that I am suspicious that these terms only serve to obscure theological issues and are suited more to a short term political strategy than to profound theological discourse. While labels provide a tempting set of catchy, alliterative tags for opponents in the present debate, they no longer shed, as once they may have done, clear light on how scripture is being understood or how scripture can offer, once again, the Bread of Life in our churches.

B. BEYOND LIBERALISM AND LITERALISM

Aside from an awareness of the dated quality of these terms and my political wariness about how they are currently used, I want to explore some other reasons why they distract us from the really important issues in the present climate of theological opinion. My further objections to the current reliance on these terms is that (1) it is ecumenically insensitive and historically naive, (2) it is elitist and misconstrues orthodoxy, and (3) it ignores the present advances in biblical and theological studies.

1. Ecumenical and Historical Problems

First, "literalism" is a misleading term to describe alleged non-liberal views of the Bible because, at a minimum, it is combative and ignores the real differences within the churches. Use of the term in the current debate panders to the prejudice that conservative evangelicals or traditionalists want to be called "literalists." An important distinction has regularly been maintained even by fundamentalists between "literal" interpretation — more colloquially, "taking the

Bible literally" — and literalistic readings that become fixed upon the isolated meaning of words or grammar at the expense of syntax, context, and semantics. Conservative evangelicals have argued consistently against literalistic interpretation. For example, Harold Lindsell in his *Battle for the Bible* does not hesitate to condemn what he calls "wooden-headed literalists."[9] On this point I would support James Barr's argument that even fundamentalists are not so much "literalists" as they are "inerrantists" who try to establish the truth of the Bible referentially and historically.[10] Conversely, we should not forget that modern historical criticism was defended and popularized in the middle of the nineteenth century in England and in the United States precisely because it allowed the interpreter more accurate historical grasp of "the literal sense" of scripture.[11] After all, the English Reformation since the sixteenth century, drawing on Continental protestant precedents, consistently argued that only the "literal sense" of scripture was normative for doctrine. So, the older protestant position served well the defense of historical criticism in the nineteenth century and had as its goal the ecumenical hope that interpreters could at last agree on the literal sense, no matter what theological differences various denominations might subsequently draw from it.

In the twentieth century, especially in the United States, we should recognize that "old liberals" and "fundamentalists" of the 1920's were both "modernists," in the sense that they shared similar modern conceptions of history and a similar modern semantic theory of author's intentionality. Modern fundamentalists were, as often as

---

9. Lindsell, Battle, p. 37. For a sophisticated investigation of these issues, see Kathleen C. Boone, *The Bible Tells Me So: The Discourse of Protestant Fundamentalism* (New York City: SUNY, 1989), pp. 39-60.

10. James Barr, *Fundamentalism* (Philadelphia: Westminster Press, 1977), p. 46.

11. For example, the famous lectures to the Scottish Presbyterian Church by W. Robertson Smith, published as *The Old Testament in the Jewish Church* (Edinburgh: Adam and Charles Black, 1931).

not, no less rationalistic or historicist in their approaches to biblical interpretation than were old liberals; old liberals were typically no less pious and idealistic than fundamentalists. I would contend that highly educated fundamentalists read the Bible no more "literalistically" than did liberal source critics. In fact, what we now commonly call "source criticism" — the search for ancient sources of the Bible: J, E, D, P, for example — was from its inception called in German *"Literaturgeschichte"* or "literary criticism," as it has been often designated in textbooks until the last few decades. If we think of both liberals and fundamentalists of this period as modernists, then we can describe fundamentalism as a response from the right wing of modernity and liberalism from the left. Fundamentalists generally sought to transform the truths of an older orthodoxy through the right wing of modernity, employing a conservative but modern form of historical-grammatical exegesis to verify the accuracy of the Bible as a referential guide to ancient historical events and, thereby, to divine revelation in history. Old liberals employed a similarly modern but more radical method of historical-critical exegesis that exposed differences between the biblical presentation of events and a modern reconstruction of the same. Because liberals usually shared with fundamentalists an assumption that the "literal" truth of scripture corresponded to an accurate perception of historical events, historical-critical insight could be used both to support as well as challenge older orthodox interpretation. The charge of "literalism" can be applied equally to both liberals and fundamentalists, depending on how we choose to weigh this ambiguous term.

A related mistake occurs when the entire pre-modern history of interpretation is presumed to offer no more than simplistic "literalism" or, worse, allegorical fantasy. Underlying this estimate of the past is a remarkably uncritical assumption that modern approaches allow interpreters to work with a clean slate, unencumbered by the impure annotations of earlier periods of interpretation. While this assumption may help justify why so few theologians can read either ecclesiastical Greek or Latin, it is a costly prejudice based on a modernist reduction of the art of interpretation itself. What scholars are now acknowledging is that prior to the modern period, interpreters frequently distinguished between the true "literal sense" of a text and what they called "the grammatical sense," including the simple referential sense of individual words or phrases which we now associate with a "literalistic" reading. In the earliest modern dictionaries of the Bible, for example, that of Augustin Calmet at the beginning of the seventeenth century, we also find a distinction made between "Le sens grammatical" as prior to the first of the classical four-fold senses, "Le sens littéral & historique." For Calmet the grammatical sense "is that which the terms of the text present to the mind," while the "literal and historical sense" is "that which pertains to history, in fact, to the narrative and to the terms of the scripture that are presented at first to the mind."[12] For Calmet the narrative context of scripture guided the reader to the "literal sense" beyond any literalistic reading associated solely with the "grammatical sense." At a minimum, we see that there is a self-conscious distinction between *literalistic* and *literal* interpretation in the pre-modern and early modern period that should be honored ecumenically and historically. Moreover, it would be theologically a dangerous mistake for "liberals" to concede that the modern "literalists" are the true bearers of the pre-modern tradition of "literal" interpretation.

It is also important that we do not identify the strong intuitive interpretations found commonly among Christian denominations and groups outside of "mainline" churches with either literalism or fundamentalism. We need to recognize that many churches — including most holiness and pentecostal groups, as well as most black and Third World churches — are not fundamentalists even though they may not regularly employ historical criticism. If we identify fundamentalism, as I have suggested, with a right wing

12. Augustin Calmet, *Distionaire de la Bible* (1730), Vol. 4, pp. 169-170.

modern historicism, then we might even think of these groups as "sub-modern." They were ostracized from the major public forums of the modern debate in the last century by reason of classism, racism, and, in some cases, both economic and educational deprivation. These groups were heavily criticized for their views of the Bible by fundamentalists and they were, just as often, ignored by liberals. The effects of modernity, nonetheless, impinged on these groups who, as it were, fed off the crumbs that fell beneath the table of privileged, primarily white and wealthy, Canadian and American culture.

At the opposite end of the class spectrum, we must also look at "post-modern" comparative literary criticism in the universities and ask how that complicates the simplistic choices between liberalism and literalism. Within the last two decades there has been unrelenting criticism of the older modern views of interpretation. In the 1970's we began to hear of "post-modern" art, literature, drama, and architecture. There is now appearing all around us a rich variety of newer "literary" approaches to the Bible that are neither literalistic nor focused on a liberal historical reconstruction of the biblical text. These approaches tend to emphasize the art and realism of the biblical text in its present form. Representative scholars outside of biblical and theological studies who have encouraged this trend include Robert Alter, Harold Bloom, Wayne Booth, Northrop Frye, and Frank Kermode. One sign of the maturity is the appearance of a volume entitled *The Literary Guide to the Bible* (1987), edited by literary critics Robert Alter and Frank Kermode. In his *Great Code of the Bible* (1981) Northrop Frye, who might easily qualify as a "liberal" in the United Church, is aware that his approach may allow people to call him a "literalist." Despite that risk he still declares, "one of the central issues of the present book [is] the 'literal' meaning."[13] He accepts the truth of this "literal" meaning which is

---

13. Northrop Frye, *The Great Code: The Bible and Literature* (New York: Harcourt Brace Janovich, 1982), p. 45.

warranted by "the shape" of the Bible itself, when "read as a unity."[14] What Frye questions is any hegemony over a criterion for the truth of the Bible that a modern historian might claim. The use of the labels "liberalism" and "literalism" will do justice neither to the pre-modern history of interpretation, to "sub-modern" Christian inter-preters, nor to some of the most articulate, late modern "literary" critics in the university.

2. The Problem of Orthodoxy

Another problem with the options of liberalism or literalism con-cerns the relation of these terms to orthodox Christian confession, and the parallel problem of implicit elitism or classism that engen-ders distrust between the formally educated and the formally unedu-cated. What lies behind the use of these terms is a proper awareness that "liberals" learned how to employ historical criticism at profes-sional colleges. "Traditionalists" or "literalists" could be identified by default as those who did not have the privilege of this new knowledge and had to rely on intuition and common sense. The church in Canada was able to avoid some of the worst effects of a public rift between "liberals" and "fundamentalists" that character-ized the crisis within the churches in the United States. In the United States, at least, "fundamentalism" cut across the social register and became part of a strong populist movement that persists even today. Here in Canada the debate over historical criticism seems to have divided fewer educational institutions and denominations, allowing, as in England, for a gradual public acceptance or tolerance of it. One reason for these circumstances may be how well in both England and Canada key proponents of the newer criticism were identified with orthodox Christian confessions. Historical criticism came to be associated with the privilege of formal education readily available to only a small portion of society. Those who were trained in modern seminaries and universities, usually in the cities, were distinguished

14. Frye, p. xiii.

14

from those, generally in rural settings, who lacked the same access to formal education. Therefore, from a Canadian perspective, there should be a constructive respect for those who continue to interpret the Bible in an older traditional manner because they have not had the opportunity to discover the rewards of modern criticism. By contrast, the situation in the United States was more often one of highly educated "fundamentalists" or conservative "evangelicals" in open public conflict with highly educated "liberals." Behind these debates was the inevitable question of who was theologically "orthodox" or heretical.

The Canadian perspective, different in many respects from that typical of the United States, shows up in Steward Crysdale's 1965 study of the United Church, *The Changing Church in Canada*. Crysdale distinguishes the major oppositions in the church as between "liberal theology" and "traditional theology." Parenthetically, I have yet to hear anyone speak of "literalistic theology." The difference between liberal and traditional theologies is that "liberals" have discovered a new freedom and flexibility in biblical interpretation due to modern criticism, while traditionalists have set their priorities on defending what "has survived with little change through many generations."[15] For this reason, Crysdale can argue that both approaches can be "orthodox" in matters of faith. This model of the conflict is generous to both sides in that traditionalist interpretation appears to be a perpetuation of pre-modern values, while "liberals" have appropriated the tools of modern science and history in a liberating, but equally faithful manner. The advantage of Crysdale's presentation is that it leaves open the question of "orthodoxy" better than the division of the situation into liberalism and literalism. A major weakness, nonetheless, is the assumption that the so-called traditionalist position simply reiterates an earlier orthodoxy. In fact, the traditionalist has transformed the older conception of orthodoxy

---

15. Stewart Crysdale, *The Changing Church in Canada* (Toronto; United Church of Canada, 1965), p. 26.

into a peculiarly modern consciousness within the right wing of the church, no less than has the liberal on the left.

The relation of liberalism to orthodoxy, of course, has its own special problems. In both Canada and the United States after World War II "neo-orthodoxy" developed as a strong criticism from within liberalism, which I have described as representing left-wing modernism. In the United States, more so than in Canada, a parallel self-critical reaction also occurred within fundamentalism — what I have called the right wing modernism — in the form of "neo-evangelicalism," associated with the success of the magazine *Christianity Today*, the formation of the National Association of Evangelicals, the public popularity of the Billy Graham crusades, and the founding of Fuller Theological Seminary. Consequently, the older "liberal theology" was no longer the primary or only defender of historical criticism. Today, the term "liberal" may most adequately signify political dispositions that can be held by believers who may represent the entire spectrum of doctrinal stances. In Canada these ambiguities are compounded by the fact that one need not be a theological "liberal" in order to support the United Church's present policy on ordination. Liberalism, however it may be defined, should not unfairly take credit for having special insight into these issues, and "old liberalism" of the 1920's was often even less open on issues of homosexuality, for example, than is the present Community of Concern within the United Church.

Let me assure you that I do not devalue many common uses of the term "liberal." I am aware, for instance, that I would be considered a liberal historical critic and a "liberal" or "radical" in most of my political perspectives. In the theological arena I am more comfortable with the adjective than the noun. I would not be a "liberal" if one takes the term to be "old liberal" in a way that ignores the strong criticisms of neo-orthodoxy in theology or post-modern criticism generally. If a liberal is anyone who is not a fundamentalist or a literalist, then I am obviously a "liberal." But, then, the label is given far more than it deserves, so I would resist its right to cover such a profound set of theological options. The more significant issue is how a non-literalistic, non-fundamentalist theology can lay claim to the orthodox heritage of confessions in the church without perpetuating either pre-modern or modern legalisms and an authoritarian inflexibility in biblical interpretation that is, in fact, alien to the Gospel itself. Moreover, as you will see, I, for one, want to reaffirm the traditional normative status of the "literal sense" of scripture.

A part of our orthodox protestant heritage which I do not want to forfeit is a conviction that the literal sense of scripture is potentially available to all believers, not just to the learned clergy. One of the most common and serious errors we face today is the implication that there are two Bibles in our churches. There is the Bible that ordinary people can see and hold in their hands and read literalistically. Then, there are the hidden reconstructed texts and historical events in which the minister or scholar can find all the really "true" sources of revelation. The layperson tries to read Genesis, but the minister preaches only from a reconstructed Yahwistic, Elohistic, or Priestly source now buried subtly, often in half and quarter verses, throughout the biblical book. The layperson tries to read Isaiah, but the minister interprets the book only as atomized into Proto-, Deutero-, and Trito-Isaiah. The layperson tries to read Matthew, but the minister orates solely on the theology of Q. As an historical critic I have no objection to historical reconstructions. However, if we succeed only in uncovering the pre-history of scripture rather than interpreting scripture itself, we will lose the basic protestant conception of the common biblical text which we all compete to illuminate.

I fear sometimes that we biblical professors in church colleges and seminaries have often been able to teach only enough about complex methods of modern historical criticism to guarantee that the minister who does not want to be called a literalist will feel guilty for the rest of his or her preaching life. If protestants once condemned

17

Roman Catholics for replacing the Bible with church magisterial traditions, we ourselves may now be accused of substituting for the common text of scripture a vast array of disputed, esoteric, but allegedly "better" texts which we scholars alone can recover and interpret. There is nothing truly "liberal," even in the best sense, about this conception of scripture. I will return to this issue subsequently, but I especially want to reject any assumption that the biblical text as we now have it cannot be sustained and interpreted without succumbing to "literalism." The challenge ought to be aimed, instead, at the historical critic to demonstrate how such esoteric knowledge increases our acuity of the text we read as Christian scripture. On the best of liberal principles we must ask ourselves how the Bible can become once again a common text of scripture in our churches, one that evokes a high and serious reading between the formally educated and formally uneducated, between the poor and the rich, between those with unjustified racial privilege and the racially disparaged, and, perhaps, even among the self-labeled "liberals," the Community of Concern, and the Renewal Fellowship in the United Church of Canada. In this respect, we would recover an older protestant principle regarding the primacy of the literal sense of scripture, a perspective so easily forfeited when options in biblical interpretation are reduced to liberalism or literalism. My hope is not for an easy reconciliation, but for a more fruitful debate over the role of scripture on the major issues of our day for the sake of the Gospel.

3. The Problem of Looking Backwards

My third objection to limiting our choices to either liberalism or literalism is that it invites neglect of recent advances in biblical studies and theology. Instead of using the perplexing questions of our day to summon us to a bold re-examination of scripture and of theology, we find ourselves reduced to political games and name-calling. Instead of harboring hope that God, through the power of the Holy Spirit, might give new life and fresh insight to our church, we

18

actually attempt to arrest our own theological development. The last two decades have seen rigorous re-examinations by biblical and theological scholars of some of the most basic issues in biblical studies and theology. These changes deserve our attention and point in some new directions beyond the older depiction of our options.

Our own period in the history of theology and biblical interpretation may prove to be one with both more confusion and promise than most in the recent past. After World War II, two major challenges or correctives to "liberal" theology virtually dominated Christian studies from the 1940's to the 1960's. In theology, a cluster of proposals associated with "realism" and its criticism of liberal "idealism" popularly came to be called "neo-orthodoxy." In biblical studies, various related confessional approaches clustered together in what became known as the Biblical Theology Movement. Histories of these movements are readily available and my purpose is not to rehearse here their major contributions. Rather, I want to take note of the evidence that both of these movements, thriving after the golden age of old liberalism, fully inherited the modern problem of how to relate truth and history. Their contributions are still felt everywhere within the contemporary theological scene, but, and this is the point I want to make, both movements lost their vigor in the 1960's, certainly by the early 1970's. In his *A Religious History of the American People*, Yale historian Sydney Ahlstrom concludes that the requiem for neo-orthodoxy occurs with J. Richard Niebuhr's *Radical Monotheism and Western Culture*, published in 1960.[16] Likewise, in his *Biblical Theology in Crisis*, Old Testament scholar Brevard Childs estimates the demise of the Biblical Theology Movement in the mid-1960's.[17]

If these interpreters of the recent history of theology are at all

16. Sydney E. Ahlstrom, *A Religious History of the American People* (New Haven: Yale Press, 1972), p. 961.

17. Brevard S. Childs, *Biblical Theology in Crisis* (Philadelphia: Westinster Press, 1970), pp. 61-87.

correct, then the present alternative to old liberalism can no longer be something called either "neo-orthodoxy" or "biblical theology." For these reasons, we find in the place of the older liberalism and neo-orthodoxy in theology, alternatives such as radical theologies, liberation theologies, revisionist theology, or cultural-linguistic models of confessional theology. In biblical studies, in the place of the Biblical Theology Movement, we find post-modern literary approaches, liberationist close readings of texts, socio-anthropological reconstructions of the ancient world, and a reformulation of the Bible as scripture. In any of the these approaches we can find a wide range of confessional postures. For example, some liberation theologians seem to advocate a "post-Christian" position while others may identify themselves as conservative "evangelicals." Little wonder that the seminal contribution of Yale theologian, George Lindbeck, called *The Nature of Doctrine* (1984) is subtitled: "Religion and Theology in a Postliberal Age." This overview is, of course, far too sketchy to do justice to any of the recent proposals. It suffices only to remind us how much the climate has changed in biblical and theological studies in the 1970's and 1980's. Those who appreciate how the entire horizon in biblical and theological studies has developed will not be satisfied with the options of liberalism, literalism, neo-orthodoxy, or traditionalism. There are clearly more fresh and exciting questions at hand for us today than those which originally informed the older liberal/literalist debate.

C. REDISCOVERING THE BIBLE AS SCRIPTURE

Neither the disciples of Jesus nor the first generation of Christians ever wanted a "New Testament." What the earliest Christians desired is clear enough — they wanted the personal return of the risen Lord, the living voice of God among them and, at the same time, the full realization of the kingdom of God on earth as well as the end of this age. They had no need of a New Testament because the scripture they shared with Jews was accepted as sufficient, alongside the preached Gospel of Jesus Christ, recollections of the words of Jesus, and various oral and written testimonies to the apostolic tradition. In these traditions they found hope that the Risen Lord, the Living Word of God, soon would be again in their midst. To many of these early Christians the delay of Christ's return must have been a disappointment second only to that of the crucifixion itself. The "New Testament" as a part of a distinctly Christian scripture was not an obvious solution to this problem.

We in the modern period easily forget that the first reference to a group of books as a "New Testament" does not occur until about

150 A.D. and finds its first known advocate in Marcion, one of the earliest heretics of the Christian church. Marcion had proposed that Christians needed a "New Testament," consisting of parts of Luke and ten Pauline Epistles, which would identify Christian scripture as separate from Jewish Scripture. He considered Jewish Scripture to be the inferior revelation of a demiurge, a lesser manifestation of the Supreme Being, and not received from the same God who revealed the Gospel through Jesus Christ and the teachings of Paul. Irenaeus, the bishop of Lyons, responded to Marcion by condemning his proposal while affirming the existence of a New Testament. Irenaeus argued for the retention of Jewish Scripture as Christian "Old Testament" and described the contents of the New Testament as follows: "the teaching of all the apostles — as given in the four Gospels and in Acts — the sayings of the Lord, and the apostolic letters of Paul."[18] Irenaeus' position probably did not seem highly contrived since these same texts had already circulated widely throughout the early churches as normative resources for preserving Christian testimony regarding the essence of the Gospel.

1. The Divine and Human Voice of Scripture

The Christian conception of the New Testament as scripture in the middle of the second century drew heavily upon an understanding of scripture inherited from Judaism. We cannot know precisely the events and pressures underlying the formation of Jewish Scriptures in the post-exilic period. However, we have some knowledge about the role of these books later within Judaism. As early as the second century B.C. in the book of Sirach (Ecclesiasticus) we have a description of the biblical resources employed by a Jewish sage — "the Torah of the Most High, ...wisdom of all the ancients, and ...

18. Hans von Campenhausen, *The Formation of the Christian Bible* (Philadelphia: Fortress Press, 1972), p. 191. He summarizes the situation, "From every side we converge on the same result: the idea and the reality of a Christian Bible were the work of Marcion, and the Church which rejected his work, so far from being ahead of him in this field, from a formal point of view, simply followed his example." (p. 148).

prophecies" (Sir. 39:1) — together with detailed examples of biblical interpretation. The prologue, written a generation later, praises the author, "my grandfather Jesus," who devoted himself to "the reading of the law (Torah) and the prophets, and the other books of our fathers." The aim of the author is to articulate "wisdom" based on biblical revelation, so that he can argue on behalf of his exposition:

> "I will again make instruction shine
> forth like the dawn,
>   and I make it shine afar;
> I will again pour out teaching like prophecy,
>   and leave it to all future generations"
>   (Sir. 24:32-33)

In these words, we hear repeated the oldest assumption that Jewish scripture is comparable to prophecy. The expositor who honors this aspect of the text should reasonably seek to offer teaching "like prophecy" based upon it. In later rabbinic debates regarding which disputed books belonged to scripture, one criterion was whether a book was "spoken by the Hòly Spirit" and whether handling the text itself would "defile the hands." The latter formulation recalls the ancient distinction between "profane" and "holy" objects which also underlies later Christian descriptions of the Bible as a "holy" or "sacred" text. Furthermore, prior to the modern period biblical books were not typically "read" in silence. Biblical Hebrew language does not even have a technical term for such a modern idea. The Hebrew word qara', most closely associated with our contemporary conception "to read," signifies more accurately "to call, to proclaim, to summon, to invite, or to read aloud." Books in general, and the Bible in particular, were normally read aloud both in private and in public; books were meant to be read in order to be overheard. For this reason Origen in the late second century could draw from the difference between the reading aloud and the hearing of a biblical text a distinction, based on an anthropological analogy, between a carnal or fleshly encounter with scripture and a grasp of its spiritual content. In any case, in the pre-modern period the written text of scripture was thought to perpetuate a living voice which the "reader" heard again when the text was read. This assumption about the voice of an ancient book, together with the Jewish conception of the Bible as a vehicle for hearing God's voice, was fully appropriated by the first followers of Jesus who frequently cited scripture with the introductory formula, "God says" or "the Holy Spirit says." Whoever seeks properly to hear the Bible as scripture inevitably seeks to hear the voice of the living God.

This pre-understanding about the nature of scripture, inherited from Judaism, was augmented in Christianity by a hellenistic conception of "inspiration." The significance of the ancient view that God is the Author of scripture has often been underestimated in the modern period, though it was accepted commonly before. For example, Matthias Flacius Illyricus, who studied with Luther and Melancthon and was a pioneer in what became the modern discipline of hermeneutics, fully recognized it. In his mid-sixteenth-century tract, *How One Should Read Holy Scripture*, Flacius writes:

> The pious man must in fact so revere the Holy Scripture and with such devotion learn to know that he reads, so to speak, no dead book neither does he penetrate the writings of still holy, revered, and wise men, but he looks for the Word of the living God himself, who right there deals with him. That one is the same as the author and he has presented it to the human race as one who always speaks directly through this book with humanity and you may learn here and there your own eternal salvation.[19]

---

19. From his *Praecepta de Ratione Legendi Sacras Literas, Nostro Arbitrio Collecta, Aut Excogitata*. For a contemporary edition see Matthias Flacius Illyricus, *De Ratione Cognoscendi Sacras Literas: Über den Erkenntnisgrund der Heiligen Schrift*, ed. by Lutz Geldsetzer (Dusseldorf: Stern-Verlag Janssen & Co., 1968), p. 88.

This common attribution of God as the author of scripture was, however, accompanied by an equally tenacious assumption that all the words of scripture were entirely human words that often could be identified with particular historical figures. We might have guessed that the last editors of the Bible, who were self-conscious that they were editing a "scripture," would have been been tempted to play down the human quality of these traditions and, thereby, to play up the idea of the Bible as superhuman communication of an eternal word from God. They did just the opposite. By means of stereotypical titles, whole books and portions of the Bible were identified with named human figures: Moses, Isaiah, David, Solomon. For example, in the early post-exilic period, editors of the biblical book of Psalms added well over a dozen titles that associated certain prayers with key events in the life of David as depicted in 2 Samuel. Later editions of the Psalms that have been found at Qumran, or in the Old Greek translation of the Psalter (LXX), in the Targums, and in Syriac versions, show an even greater number of such historicizing titles, exploring further the biographical connection between David and individual psalms. So it is that a recognition of the human character of the words of scripture belongs to the very process by which scripture itself is recognized as the revealed word of God. We might observe here that Jewish scripture, in contrast to scriptures in most other world religions, presents us with a thoroughly human witness to the living voice of God. The words of the biblical text can offer at most a prophetic-like witness to the Word of God. In scripture, at least, God summons us by means of words uttered by people who are no more likely bearers of divine truth than you or I.

2. The Modern Conception of Scriptures in Religion

These reflections on the earliest expectations regarding the words of scripture cause us to examine how our views of the Bible as scripture have changed over time up to the modern period. Our

English word "Bible" harks back to the earlier Greek plural form "tá biblía," "the books," which in the common parlance of the Middle Ages was almost entirely superceded by a singular latinate form, "biblia," that is, "book" or "Bible," a synonym of the Latin "scriptura" meaning "a writing." A precedent for using the word "scripture" or "scriptures" can be found in New Testament references to the common Jewish Bible as "he grapé," "the writing," or "hai graphaí," "the whole collection of writings." Though the Bible had been called "canonical" earlier, from the fourth century on "the Bible" or the term "Bible" was regarded as synonymous with "the canon." The term "canon" is a semitic loan word with the double sense of both being a norm, ideal, or standard, and comprising a fixed collection or delimited corpus of books. Before the modern period, Christian references to the Bible carried an additional association of being a book or books given by God and we commonly find God or the Holy Spirit mentioned as its Author. Not until the nineteenth century in the West was the idea adopted that the Bible was something which a group of men and women "had chosen" for themselves as authoritative and to which they had assigned a special status. Before the nineteenth century we might say that Christians thought that the Bible and God as its author had chosen them, rather than the other way around.

In any case, the preferred high cultural term for the Bible at the beginning of the nineteenth century was "scripture." By the beginning of the twentieth century this use of the word "scripture" was extended beyond the Judaeo-Christian tradition as a designation to describe the primary religious documents in other religions as well. An example of this shift was the repeated publication of Max Müller's *The Sacred Books of the East*, first published in 1879, which went through various reprints in the twentieth century under titles such as "The Scriptures of the World".[20] Comparative religionist William Cantwell Smith has been among the most perceptive critics to point out how this twentieth century use of the term "scripture" implied an objectification of the texts of scriptures, which in turn supported the assumption that a modern historical study of their pre-histories would disclose what they really "meant." In a seminal essay in 1971, "The Study of Religion and the Study of the Bible," and again in 1980 in a brilliant, often overlooked, presentation, "The True Meaning of Scripture: An Empirical Historian's Nonreduction-ist Interpretation of the Qur'an," Smith challenged religionists to refine how they assessed religious interpretations of scriptures.[21] He emphasized that a text of scripture is not simply an "object," a fixed cluster of historical data open to detached scientific analysis. By its very nature, the content of Jewish and Christian scripture includes its revelatory purpose and this capacity of a scripture can be described only in relationship to a specific, historical community of believers.

From a study of comparative religions, we might accept the generalization that scriptures by their nature invoke a reading in pursuit of a transcendent truth, revelation, word, or even the living voice of God. A method of interpretation not in service to this goal, no matter how significant historically or how much it is considered essential to modern understanding, should not be confused with a reading of these texts as *scripture*. Smith even dares to suggest that we think about all scriptures in world religions "from God's point of view" so that we "see God as using scripture more or less successfully in the ongoing endeavor to salvage human beings from sin and despair and to invite us to higher realms, of truth and love."[22] Though I am less confident (and less competent) than Smith in my ability to describe the role of God throughout world religions, I find that his formulation impressively employs the logic of the left wing of modernity against

---

20. I owe much of these insights to Wilfred Cantwell Smith and especially his unpublished lecture, "Scripture: Issues as Seen by a Comparative Religionist," given at Claremont Graduate School, March 14, 1985. That lecture will be a chapter in a forthcoming book of his on scripture, from a comparativist perspective.

21. JAAR 39/2 (1971) 131-140 and *International Journal of Middle East Studies* 11 (1980) 487-505.

22. Smith, see n. 20.

some of modernity's own naiveties about how to read scripture. We miss the scriptural dimension of scriptures whenever we treat them merely as lifeless artifacts. We may succeed only in performing scientific or historical autopsies upon scriptural texts, preparing them, with the help of aesthetic criticism, for a decent, modern burial. From a purely humanistic standpoint, the question of how to read the Bible as scripture requires that we carefully consider the rules of exposition by which these texts become the Bread of Life for a community of believers.

Of course, the Bible has been, and will continue to be, read in a great, perhaps infinite, variety of ways. These various readings of the Bible coincide with an equally diverse set of expectations on the part of different readers. My concern here is not to argue that there is only one proper way to read a book, much less the Bible. I encourage my students to learn as many methods and interpretive skills as they can. The challenge is enormous. It is an asset to know the languages in which a book is written, including cognate languages and issues of syntax, the general history and the originating socio-anthropological and economic milieu of a text, and, also, source, form, traditio-historical and redaction criticism, and the equally complex range of literary criticism from, for example, the fastidious intentionality theory of E. D. Hirsh to rhetorical, New Literary, structuralist, and deconstructionist approaches. I am aware that different methods, like spectacles of differing foci and acuity, presuppose different visions of texts so that the pragmatic perception of the allegedly same text will, in fact, vary from method to method. My response to the great variety of methods, each with its own pragmatic vision of a text may be expressed metaphorically by recalling the words of the Apostle Paul in 1 Cor. 6:12, "All things are lawful for me, but not all things are helpful." My choice of interpretive strategies does not depend on any decision about the moral or theological legitimacy of the methods themselves. Instead, I want to ask a pragmatic and eco-nomic question — how will these methods and their results help me both to sustain a particular vision of this text and to illuminate it? In this framing of the question, I am not precluding the value of other possible readings of the Bible.

Despite acknowledging that a reading of the Bible as a scripture is only one among many possibilities, it can be argued that such an interpretation is far from an arbitrary imposition on the biblical text. On both literary and historical-critical grounds we may argue that "the shape" of the Bible as we have it corresponds editorially to its function as scripture. While Northrop Frye argues this case on grounds of the literary anatomy of the text itself, Brevard Childs and other recent biblical scholars, including myself, argue for it also from the evidence of how the biblical books were historically formed. My own work has concentrated on the indications within the text of how editors in the late stages of the formation of biblical books registered their assumptions that these books belong together within a common intertext of scripture. Their "canon conscious redactions" provide explicit warrants for an interpretation of once independent books together as a witness to the same subject matter: the Torah of God, the Word of God as prophetic promise and judgment, the Wisdom of God, and, for Christian scripture, the Gospel of Jesus Christ. Therefore, our appeal to the Bible as scripture is not simply an arbitrary "functionalist" position, but claims to honor the actual form of the Bible itself. It is precisely this characteristic form and function of scripture that the modern period has most easily forgotten in its rich application of historical and literary methods. By neglecting this form and function of scripture, theologians who use historical criticism, on the one hand, often fall prey to the temptation of venturing only pious interpretations of reconstructed historical events in the pre-history of the Bible, instead of offering robust historical and theological interpretation of a constructed scripture. On the other hand, scholars who use primarily literary-aesthetic approaches often miss the religious dimension of the Bible entirely by focusing only on isolated elements or structural features within the text as a whole.

Wilfred C. Smith has expressed this dilemma in a cogent aphorism: Modern historical critical methods have taught us how to read the Bible pre-biblically, while modern "Bible as literature" approaches teach us how to read the Bible post-biblically. The only thing we no longer know how to do is to read the Bible biblically.

3. The Semantic Transformation from Ancient Traditions to Scripture

When we think about Jewish and Christian scripture in modern historical terms and, by analogy, to "scripture" in other religions, we discover that they share a remarkable feature in common. With the exception of Mani and the Manichaen scriptures in the fourth century A.D., the designated human authors of scriptures in all of the major world religions did not originally think they were writing scripture. Their prophecies, wisdom, advice, dreams, and hymns became recognized as "scripture" later, in ways that exceeded their original intents. So, in the Old Testament, parts of a pre-scriptural hymn book of Solomon's temple now belong to the biblical book of Psalms and are read as Jewish and Christian scripture rather than as merely ancient hymnology within Israelite religion. So, too, in the New Testament the Apostle Paul cites "scripture" within his letters, but never claims that his letters are the same as scripture. He even distinguishes carefully in his letters between his own apostolic authority and what is his own opinion ("not from the Lord"). When the ancient hymns of Israel and Paul's missionary letters have become scripture, they are read within the framework of a new context of scripture and, therefore, their meaning and significance as literature is changed as well.

A failure to recognize this point accounts for one of the most common historical fallacies in historical criticism during the twentieth century, namely, the assumption that every text which can be reconstructed in the pre-history of the Bible should be called a "biblical tradition." More often than not, reconstructed traditions, such as the Yahwistic or Elohistic source in the Old Testament, are technically "pre-biblical" traditions which independently never had any status as "scripture" in ancient Israel. This circumstance perhaps becomes most obvious if we consider those "canaanite" psalms that probably derive from earlier Baalistic hymns (e.g. Psalm 29). In these cases the problem in describing the original Baalistic hymns as "biblical tradition" is obvious. The fallacy is compounded when "biblical theology" is taken to be the cumulative result of the religious content of such "biblical tradition."

The same error is apparent in the recent effort by James Barr to distinguish a praiseworthy "biblical faith" from a pejoratively assessed "scriptural religion."[23] At the outset, this modern use of the idea of "a faith," typically more a Christian than a Jewish expression, already betrays an orientation toward religion that presupposes a relationship between canonical norms and a community of believers. Still, we might presume by this formulation to be able to distinguish, for example, the authentic "biblical faith" of the historical Amos from the inauthentic "scriptural religion" of those who interpret the book of Amos. But, of course, Amos did not have a Bible, so he could not logically be said to have a "biblical faith" at all. This judgment does not deny that his beliefs may have been exemplary and true, from the later standpoint of scripture. Conversely, we can argue that only certain aspects of Amos' religious beliefs have been later taken up into a "biblical faith" by virtue of their survival and transformation within the composition of the scriptural book of Amos. Certainly, Judaism did not declare as normative all that the historical Amos ever said, did, or thought. In this respect, the Bible alone provides us with a presentation of Amos as a witness to biblical revelation without either reducing the subject matter of scripture to the historical Amos or portraying "Amos' faith" itself as a norm of either Jewish or Christian faith. For these reasons, we might want to

23. James Barr, *Holy Scripture: Canon, Authority, Criticism* (Philadelphia: Westminster Press, 1983), p. 2, 12, 21.

distinguish more carefully, in the light of modern historical criticism, between pre-biblical religious convictions and biblical/scriptural religious beliefs or faith.

The semantic transformation that takes place when pre-biblical traditions become a part of a scripture can be highly significant. Raymond Brown has recently discussed some of these implications for how we now view and read the Gospels as "books" in the New Testament. Only Mark contains the term "gospel" originally in its introduction, so that the designation of four different books as "Gospels" reflects an adaptation of them within the context of scripture.[24] Luke prefers to describe his work not as a "gospel" but as "a narrative" (1:1) and the opening lines of what we now call Acts clearly assumed that Luke and Acts were Books I and II of a single work which would not likely have been described as a "Gospel." However, the formation of scripture includes the separation of Luke from Acts by the "Gospel" of John. Since Luke depended on Mark and sought to tell the story of God's revelation by including the activity of the apostles together with the life of Jesus, Brown observes, "The canonical process has, in a sense, undone his intent."[25] Put another way, whatever was the original intent of Luke, the first volume is now an independent torso, read as one "Gospel" witness among three others. The four together bear testimony to the one Gospel of Jesus Christ. Scripture invites us to read the "Gospel" Luke as a Gospel in a context not originally intended by Luke its author. A special intertext is established for Luke among the Gospels and in that form alone it has the form and function of a New Testament "book" of scripture within Christianity. This change in context of Luke within the New Testament corresponds to a subtle but significant shift in the semantic import of Luke as a biblical "Gospel," distinct

24. Cf. Henry Cadbury, *Luke-Acts* (London, SPCK, 1968), p. 10, "These four books, whatever their original name, came to be known collectively or individually by the work 'gospel'... and in varying order were always transmitted as a single group."

25. Raymond Brown, *The Critical Meaning of the Bible* (New York: Paulist Press, 1981), p. 31.

from its earlier role as Book I in Luke's original two volume work.

Similarly, we recognize that the earliest Pauline Epistles were letters composed before the Gospels were written. Some of the original letters were left independent or edited together, conjoined later to what we in the modern period have called "Deutero-Pauline" letters. We might say that the Deutero-Pauline letters present us historically with Paul as though he had read the Gospels. Regardless, the entire collection of Pauline Letters are now set after the four Gospels and Acts. Both the written Gospels and the Pauline Epistles are read despite these historical differences as commentary on each other and read together as a collective human witness to the *one Gospel of Jesus Christ.* A modern critical understanding of the formation of the New Testament allows us to recognize some of these semantic transformations that have taken place as pre-biblical traditions became a part of a later Christian Bible. From this perspective a modern historical reconstruction of a genuine Pauline letter does not in itself provide us with a text that is better suited to be scripture. Such a reconstruction may actually de-scripturalize the biblical text with which it begins by attempting to recover only its pre-scriptural form and context. Even modern critical speculation about what were the original words of Jesus can reconstruct, at most, a pre-scriptural level which *in esse* has no independent authority as scriptural revelation. The greater historical accuracy of a tradition does not guarantee in itself any greater capacity of that tradition to function as scripture. The very nature of scripture entails a presumption that places all such human history under judgment according to a quite different, transcendent, norm or point of view.

4. The Literal Sense of Scripture

These insights regarding the history and nature of the Bible have led to a rigorous re-examination of what was intended by the traditional view of "the literal sense" of scripture. Scholars involved with these issues work in a wide range of different fields, from church history, to theology, to biblical studies, to comparative literature (e.g., Northrop Frye), to comparative religions (Wilfred C. Smith). Certainly when the Reformers sought to "restore the Gospel," they argued directly from the Greek and Latin Fathers that only the literal sense of scripture was normative for Christian doctrine. Just how basic this notion is can be seen in the response of William Whitaker in the 1550's to the Roman Catholic "Counter Reformation," associated with the Council of Trent in 1545. By the mid-sixteenth century both the protestant and Roman Catholic positions had matured. Now the English protestants, at some geographical distance from the worst acrimony commonplace among the Lutheran scholastics, sought to refine their own position regarding the role of scripture. Whitaker could state that he agreed even with Thomas Aquinas that only the literal sense of scripture was a proper basis for establishing Christian doctrine. He argued that the mistake within church tradition had been to think of the other uses of scripture in the classical four-fold senses (i.e., the tropological, anagogical, and allegorical) as "senses" at all. Whitaker insisted that only the literal was a true sense of scripture while these other modes of interpretation were, at best, only uses and applications of the literal.[26] In this debate in the late Reformation or early modern period, we see that at least protestants and Roman Catholics agreed on the primacy of the literal sense. Just as a consciousness of new literary-rhetorical insights into the Bible during the period of the Reformation fueled a fresh debate over the literal sense of scripture, so our knowledge of historical criticism has affected how we can define the literal sense of scripture today. We in the modern period can reaffirm old truths of Christian faith best if we are able to show how new knowledge of history and literature can give us greater precision in our ability to interpret the Bible biblically. For the limited purposes of these

---

26. William Whitaker, *A Disputation on Holy Scripture* [1610] (London: Johnson Reprint, reprint from the Parker Society series, 1968), pp. 408-9.

essays, I want to summarize some key aspects in the present redis-covery and reformulation of the literal sense of scripture.

5. Jewish Scripture and the Old Testament/Midrash and Literal Sense

The predominant Christian emphasis on the literal sense as the normative or canonical sense of scripture is neither simply inherited from Judaism nor narrowly based on evidence of New Testament use of the Old Testament. A comparison between Judaism and Christi-anity shows how different priorities in biblical interpretation devel-oped between the two religions. Within Judaism the central subject matter of scripture is clearly "the Torah." The word "Torah" includes both "law" and "teaching" of God. The prophetic portions of the Bible and the writings (including especially the "wisdom" books of Solomon) were described by rabbis as "fences" around the Torah, protecting it from misinterpretation and providing commentary upon it.[27] After the destruction of the Herodian temple in 70 A.D., we see the formation of the Mishnah, which attained closure as a book in about 200 A.D. From about 400 A.D. in rabbinic Judaism we find the redaction of the Palestinian Talmud so that the Mishnah and the Talmud (including, later, the so-called Babylonian Talmud) came to be called "Oral Torah" as distinguished from the "Written Torah" of scripture. Both the Oral Torah and the Written Torah were normative sources of God's revelation; the former was thought to transmit the oral teaching of Moses given privately at Sinai to the elders, while the latter came directly from Moses in written form to the people. Only the Written Torah — Jewish Scripture — could "defile the hands" which indicated its special status over all of other torah traditions.[28] Nevertheless, the existence of a normative Oral Torah parallel to Jewish Scripture as Written Torah helps to explain why most Jewish

27. Cf. Jacob Neusner, *Torah: From Scroll to Symbol in Formative Judaism* (Philadelphia; Fortress Press, 1985).

religious interpretation of scripture traditionally employs a dynamic form of interpretation called "midrash." Generations before the closure of the Mishnah, rabbis had already begun to develop rules to govern midrashic interpretation. While rabbis have preferred midrashic exposition to the plain sense or "peshat" of the biblical text, they did not completely ignore the plain sense or deny its importance as a check at times on the midrashic.

In some respects, the hermeneutical situation within Judaism differs radically from that of Christianity. By adding a New Testament to Jewish scripture, Christians transformed the semantic import of the Jewish Scripture into a preceding or "Old" Testament and two highly significant shifts occurred. First, Christians claimed that the subject matter of the entire Christian scripture, not just the New Testament, was the Gospel of Jesus Christ. The relation of the Gospel to the Torah became a major issue debated both internally within the New Testament and within later Christian theology. Second, unlike the Jewish Oral Torah, the New Testament was added to an already existing scripture, extending instead of running parallel to it. Christianity is the only major world religion to form its scripture by such a "piggyback" canon. The resulting Christian scripture, a combination of Old and New Testaments, appears as one long literary horizon without clearly defined extra-biblical norms. This formation of the Christian Bible naturally lends itself to narrative and figural literary interpretation. Likewise, the divided nature of Christianity may also help explain why arguments about doctrine readily became associated with debates over the plain or literal sense of the text. We must acknowledge that some interpreters, such as Origen, have treated the literal sense as only an elementary aspect of scripture, a "carnal" or "fleshly" sense in contrast to a more sophisticated attainment of its soul or spirit. Moreover, the elements constitutive of the literal sense of scripture have necessarily changed

28. Sid Z. Leiman, *The Canonization of Hebrew Scripture* (Hamden: Archon Books, 1976), pp. 102ff.

over time as new ideas about grammar, syntax, semantics, and history influenced each generation of interpreters. More often than not, modern scholars fail to appreciate the earlier attempts at literal interpretation, condemning them as merely intuitive or, worse, "allegorical." This modern dismissal of pre-modern "literal" interpretation is often due to an assumption that modern historical data is the only criterion of a text's factual content or realism. How to interpret the history of biblical interpretation is itself a central issue and very complex. For our purposes, we need only observe that the literal sense became recognized throughout the pre-modern period as the primary doctrinal sense of Christian scripture, without depreciating the practical value of various "spiritual" types of interpretation. I want to argue that we need to rediscover a critical understanding of the literal sense of scripture as a common ground once more, for all of us, especially within the present controversies of the United Church.

These comments have some practical implications for how our churches currently cite the biblical lessons in a Sunday morning service. It is common in many congregations of the United Church to refer to the Old Testament lesson as "Hebrew Scripture" alongside the New Testament. I have heard of one church that refers to these two lessons as "Hebrew Scripture" and "Christian Scripture." In either case, the selectivity of the passage cited as "Hebrew Scripture" as well as its association with the New Testament, rather than Oral Torah, betrays the fact that it is used as a part of Christian scripture, that is to say, as "Old Testament." As shown earlier, the literal interpretation of Old Testament with the Gospel as its subject matter can be quite different from a Jewish interpretation of Hebrew or Jewish scripture. The Christian use of the Old Testament is related to but is not the same as an interpretation that honors the integrity of Jewish Scripture. Jews have every right to challenge Christians by stating that the Christian use of the Old Testament has altered its significance. Note that even the common order of Jewish scripture concludes with the edict of Cyrus in 2 Chronicles and the promise to Jews of a return to the land, while the Christian Old Testament concludes with Malachi and a potentially messianic promise of the return of Elijah (Mal. 4:5- 6). Christians, in my view, can justify such a transformation of Jewish Scripture only by a scandalous claim of new revelation in the life, death, and resurrection of Jesus Christ. For that reason, Christians should not presume to interpret Jewish Scripture for Jews, as though all of our Christian theological assessments of the Old Testament ought to be necessary implications of the Bible from a Jewish perspective.

6. The Subject Matter of Christian Scripture

A basic rule integral to the literal nature of the Bible *as scripture* is that within its literal sense the interpreter must be able to hold the text together with its subject matter. We noted that the Torah is the principal subject matter of Judaism and that for Christianity it is the Gospel of Jesus Christ. If we keep this rule in mind, we will find that our effort to discern the literal sense of the biblical text will vary with the capacity of the specific texts themselves to bear witness to that subject matter. Some texts seem richly suited to this appropriation of scripture and have become known as key "loci" (places) or *dicta probantia* upon which most doctrinal debates tend to center. There is also an awareness that some texts can thwart our interpretive desires, so that Augustine and others early in the history of interpretation did not hesitate to acknowledge the possibility that some texts may not have a literal sense as *scripture*. For example, the words in the conquest stories of Joshua are plain enough, though their literal sense or peshat to Christians and Jews respectively was another matter. Neither Jews nor Christians were willing to accept uncritically these accounts of the total annihilation of conquered people as a literal witness to the Torah or the Gospel. Jewish midrashic interpretation subordinated these stories to the clearer teaching of the Torah. In Christian tradition these texts, and others lacking an explicit literal sense, were as a rule spiritualized through non-literal interpretations in order to keep them before us and to make them useful in matters of faith. Flaccius' pastoral advice was that we memorize in particular such texts and pray that the Holy Spirit might help us find a way to understand them literally. After all, the problem may be our limited acuity rather than what he calls "alien" and "false" elements in the text itself. There is always the possibility that a text which does not seem to have a literal sense for one generation may be viewed in a different light by another. Nonetheless, the principle that the literal sense must envision the text as a witness to its subject matter corresponds to the most basic definition of the Bible as a scripture.

Besides recognizing the principal subject matter of Jewish and Christian scripture as the Torah or the Gospel, we need to consider how other key idioms of scripture play an important role. Jews in the time of Jesus often described the scripture as either "the law and the prophets" or "the law, prophets, and writings."[29] Within the divisions of Jewish scripture we find blocks of literature associated with certain figures who are identified with particular idioms of revelation. So, Moses is presented in association with the Torah. The note at the end of Deuteronomy that says no prophet will arise who is superior to him guarantees that his account of the Torah cannot be supplanted by any later prophetic claims. Next we find "the Prophets" who, unlike Moses, do not know God "face to face," but whose prophetic word is an idiom of revelation complementing the revelation of the Torah through Moses. Finally, in 1 Kings 3, Solomon is presented as receiving the gift of wisdom from God and he is described, in language similar to that of Moses, as the sage *par excellence*: "none like you has been before and none like you shall arise after you" (v.12). As the Mosaic books within scripture demarcate the essentials of the Torah and the prophetic books circumscribe

---

29. Walter Zimmerli, *The Law and the Prophets* (New York: 1967).

the prophetic word, so the Solomonic books epitomize a divinely given wisdom (cf. Prov. 2:6; 30:1-6). My point is that within Jewish Scripture, torah, prophecy, and wisdom become key idioms of biblical revelation. So, Judaism debates the relation of torah to wisdom, or how the later prophecy provides commentary on the torah. Christianity inherits these idioms from Judaism and in the written Gospels, Jesus is presented as one greater than Moses, the prophets, or Solomon, one who employs and fulfills each of these idioms in the age of the Messiah. Outside the written Gospels of the New Testament, these same older bibical idioms are again taken up so that prophecy and wisdom of the earlier dispensation are now further expanded in Christian apostolic and prophetic teaching (e.g., the Pauline Epistles and the book of Revelation), together with Christian forms of wisdom (e.g., in the teaching of Jesus, in various Pauline epistles and especially in the book of James). Hence, the challenge posed by the New Testament is to account for how the Gospel incorporates or fulfills the prior revelation in the Old Testament of God's torah, prophecy, and wisdom. This topic permeates the language of faith within the New Testament itself and constitutes a major theme of Christian scripture. Its implications continue to be felt through the entire history of Christian interpretation. For example, how the law and wisdom are related in any expression of Jewish or Christian ethics remains a common question for both religions. The relation of the Gospel to law continues to be debated among Christians precisely because of the claims and ambiguities perpetuated by the literal sense of scripture itself. The implications of this understanding of scripture touch on the basic matters of how a Bible study is conducted and how the scripture is preached each Sunday morning. According to this description, preaching could be described as the effort to interpret the literal sense of scripture according to the witness of its subject matter, the Gospel, and in the light of various biblical idioms of revelation: the law of God, God's promise and judgment, and the wisdom of God.

7. Biblical Realism and Historical Reference

More than any other study, Hans Frei's *Eclipse of Biblical Narrative: A Study in Eighteenth and Nineteenth Century Hermeneutics*
(1974) endeavors to reformulate and to rediscover the realism that is
a necessary element of the literal sense in scripture. He demonstrates
how the realistic element of scripture has been lost whenever the
meaning of the text becomes associated with its potential to refer to
some realm of the really real outside of the text, whether that realm
is a modern conception of history, transcendent ideas, or the psychological interiority of the reader. Relying on the model of mimetic
realism as advocated by comparative literary scholar, Eric Auerbach,
Frei has been able to demonstrate how biblical traditions make a
tyrannical claim about the nature of reality through the art of realistic
cumulative depiction. Biblical texts commonly foreground a description of human activity in a manner that leaves them "fraught
with psychological background." In order to make sense of such
history-like narratives, the reader is predisposed to participate in the
biblical construction of reality so that a reader renders herself or
himself as a figure in the depictive universe of the text. In this way
the text both depicts a universal reality in the full particularity and
concreteness of a specific narrative account, and renders the reality
of the reader in the course of its interpretation. We realize also that
scripture presents this realism as a divine revelation. The reader by
faith employs this realistic depiction with its own language of faith
in order to label and define the reality of her or his own situation. The
Bible as scripture becomes a touchstone to reality, allowing the
interpreter to make sense of contemporary experiences and ideas
from God's point of view. George Lindbeck has further developed
this line of argument in connection with a cultural linguistic model
of Christian theology and world religions.[30] These proposals repre-

---

30. George A. Lindbeck, *The Nature of Doctrine: Religion and Theology in a Postliberal Age*
(Philadelphia: Westminster Press, 1984), pp. 46-72.

sent a strong challenge to referential theories of interpretation and to pious applications of modern historicism to scripture, often including those popularly described as liberal and literalist. Frei and Lindbeck have helped us gain a new appreciation for both how we interpret the literal sense of scripture theologically in terms of its realism and how such an interpretation implies that scripture, in turn, begins to interpret us.

My principal criticism of Hans Frei's work is that he attributes too much significance to "narrative" in exploring biblical realism. Narrative is not the decisive term in the particular periods he closely examines. My suspicion is that his effort to displace a modern historicism tempted him to emphasize its literary counterpart, realistic narrative. Moreover, Frei's use of Auerbach, a master of serious modern realism in nineteenth-century Victorian novels, has further disposed him to talk about realistic elements of narrative as though they belong to a formal property of the narratives themselves. Such a realistic reading of scripture seems warranted far more generally by scripture so that the reader searches for the realistic element even among the unrealistic parts — even aesthetically low or comic traditions — of scripture. The realistic element is, therefore, a general capacity rather than a particular property of a particularly efficacious genre of scripture. These reservations are compounded by Frei's inadequate treatment of the role of historical criticism in his proposal.

8. The Scope, Shape, or Canonical Context of Scripture

In the work of Brevard Childs, Rolf Rendtorff, Raymond Brown, and a number of other scholars, including myself, there has appeared since the 1970's a new effort to describe what Childs was the first to call the "canonical context" of scripture. In the following pages, I will illustrate the implications of this manner of describing the intertextual form and function of scripture, what Childs has called "the shape" of biblical books. Prior to the nineteenth century interpreters such as Calvin and Luther often spoke of the "pattern" or "design" of a scriptural text. However, from the middle of the sixteenth century in Europe, and, especially among English protestants from the beginning of the seventeenth, we hear predominantly of the "scope" of biblical books.[31] This pre-modern appeal to the "scope" of books looked to titles, beginnings and endings, as well as to key topic repetitions and summaries in books. The term itself had been employed as early as the fourth century by Athanasius in his refutation of the Arians and has other counterparts back to the time of Irenaeus. My point is that through modern historical criticism we are rediscovering aspects of the context of scripture and internal warrants in the Bible for reading it as scripture, that had been overlooked or ignored earlier in modernity.

Early modern historical critics failed to appreciate what had been called the "scope" of biblical texts precisely because of how they came to understand the common assumption in the church that the literal sense of scripture is the same as the biblical author's intent. As we shall see, older critical approaches failed to distinguish adequately between the effective presentation of a "biblical" author — e.g., Moses, David, Isaiah, or Paul — and a modern conception of them as historical persons. In fact, the traditional association of the literal sense with the author's intent was used by historical critics to justify the use of modern methods in Bible study. In the older period, the assumption was that the scope of a text would be complemented by appealing to the biblical author's intent rather than the reverse, that the reconstruction of a historical author's intent would determine the meaning of a biblical text and reduce the older conception of the

---

31. For general guides to a canonical context or composition historical approaches, see respectively, Brevard S. Childs, *Introduction to the Old Testament as Scripture* (Philadelphia: Fortress, 1979) and Rolf Rendtorff, *The Old Testament: An Introduction* (Philadelphia: Fortress, 1986). On the conception of "scope," see Gerald T. Sheppard, "Between Reformation and Modern Commentary: The Perception of the Scope of Biblical Books," pp. xlii-li, in William Perkins, *A Commentary on Galatians [1617] with Introductory Essays*, ed. Gerald T. Sheppard (New York: The Pilgrim Press, 1989).

scope of a text to merely the author's purpose within that historically reconstructed intentionality.[32] The importance of the canonical context lies in its recovery of what earlier generations sought to identify with the term "scope." The crucial role of this descriptive dimension to scripture is shown by the rules of Flacius. He identifies the first things one should detect in a scripture: its "scope, purpose, and intent." According to Flacius, by ascertaining the scope of a text, the distribution of its parts, and its argument in relation to the analogy of faith (the subject matter of scripture), we can be assured in reading scripture:

> By these things you will be prevented from, as it were, wandering lost in a forest or from sailing and travelling in a dark night, not knowing where (you are) or in what direction you are turned, and where you are going: But you will know where you are, and where you are going: where is for you east, west, north and south: (just) how far away or near you are from a certain river, mountain, valley, or precipice.

With this hope about how we journey through scripture, we will next move to the book of Psalms and, then, through some of the most uncharted territory in the Old Testament, the biblical wisdom books of Proverbs, Ecclesiastes, and Song of Songs, attributed to Solomon.[33]

---

32. See Brevard S. Childs, "The Sensus Literalis of Scripture: an Ancient and Modern Problem," pp. 80-95, *Beiträge zur Alttestamentlichen Theology* [FS Walter Zimmerli], ed. H. Donner, R. Hanhart, and R. Smend (Göttingen: Vandenhoeck & Ruprecht, 1976) and especially Robert Bruce Robinson, *Roman Catholic Exegesis Since Divino Afflante Spiritu: Hermeneutical Implications* (Atlanta: Scholars Press, 1988), p. 24.

33. For a more detailed treatment of the formation of the Jewish Scripture and implications for religious interpretation, see Gerald T. Sheppard, "Canonization: Hearing the Voice of the Same God Through Historically Dissimilar Traditions," *Interpretation* 34/1 (1982) pp. 21-33.

II

PSALMS:
HOW DO THE
ORDINARY WORDS
OF WOMEN AND MEN
BECOME GOD'S WORD
TO ME?

A. INTRODUCTION

The question that forms the title of this section was first posed by Dietrich Bonhoeffer and epitomizes a profoundly modern question about the Bible. He observes:

> The Holy Scripture is the Word of God to us. But the prayers are the words of men. How do the prayers then get into the Bible? Let us make no mistake about it, the Bible is the Word of God even in the Psalms. Then are these prayers to God also God's own word? That seems rather hard to grasp.[1]

These questions are modern because the inference behind them is that David may not be the historical author, and that, therefore, these prayers are composed of ordinary words not originally intended to be scripture. Prior to the modern period most Christians would have framed the question quite differently. As illustrated in

---

1. Dietrich Bonhoeffer, *Psalms: the Prayer Book of the Bible* (Minneapolis: Augsburg Publishing House, 1970), p. 13.

Martin Luther's lengthy exposition on "the last words of David" found in 2 Samuel 23:1-3, earlier Christians could simply identify David as a prophet (see, also, NT) and as the author of the book of the Psalms.[2] Therefore, the biblical book of psalms could be viewed as deriving historically both from the articulate words of David, "the sweet psalmist of Israel" (2 Sam. 23:1), and from the inspired words of David, through whom "the Spirit of the Lord speaks" (v. 2). The prayers of David could be read as prophecies even as these words of David also modeled in form and content how one ought to pray.

---

2.   Martin Luther, "A Treatise on the Last Words of David," pp. 265-352, in *Luther's Works*, Vol. 15, ed. Jaroslav Pelikan (Saint Louis: Concordia Publishing, 1972).

B. THE MODERN PROBLEM

The rise of modern criticism devastated this older historical alliance between David and the book of Psalms. First, modern critics drew attention to the fact that many psalms are not ascribed to David. There are only about thirteen psalms (e.g. Psalms 3, 18, 51, 52) in the received Hebrew text of Psalms which are, by their titles, linked specifically to events in the life of David, but almost all of these follow the same stylized pattern and probably derive from post-exilic times. There are many untitled psalms and many assigned to other biblical figures, including one to Moses (90) and two to David's son, Solomon (72; 127). Psalm 72 concludes with an editorial notation, "the prayers of David, son of Jesse, are ended"; nonetheless, many other psalms assigned to David can be found among those that follow. Many of these features had been observed by pre-modern Jewish and Christian interpreters, but the implications for a reconstruction of the psalms separate from the historical life of David remained unexplored. Once the biblical presentation of David lost historical support in the modern period, the question Bonhoeffer asked could be framed as it is, without any reference to David at all.

A second consequence of modern psalm study belongs to an exciting discovery about the actual origins of the ancient traditions preserved by the book of Psalms. Initially, biblical critics tried to apply source criticism to the psalms under the assumption that each unit of tradition represented the written artistry of a highly educated poet. It was widely held that these poems dated from the post-exilic period when writing became a dominant mode of individual expression. However, nineteenth-century investigations into the nature of folklore and fairy tales pointed in a new direction. In a pioneering study of the biblical psalms Hermann Gunkel demonstrated that most of them derive from oral rather than written compositions and were orchestrated according to rules of poetic beauty. These aesthetic rules of oral composition probably remained unconscious in the minds of the psalmists. For a proper appreciation of the psalms Gunkel proposed an aesthetic investigation, one part of which was later called "form criticism," that classified psalms according to their particular form and social function. He emphasized the sociological dimension in the origin of the psalms so that they were categorized into types such as laments, thanksgiving, hymns, spiritual songs, and so forth. Gunkel held that these oral psalms were later subjected to crude editorial additions when they were written down. The activity of writing down these oral prayers introduced an artificiality and sacrificed the vitality of the original utterances. Editors in subsequent generations would seek to overcome these problems by employing equally artificial additions. By observing typical elements within the original oral psalms, Gunkel hoped to recover the intellectual and spiritual assumptions undergirding the work of the ancient psalmists. From the typical elements, he sought to retrieve precious information, inadvertently preserved in the prayers, relevant to a history of Israelite religion. Gunkel considered this effort to be the primary goal of a biblical scholar. Furthermore, the result of this examination of ancient religious life and beliefs belonged to what

Gunkel called a "history of piety" (*Frömmigkeitsgeschichte*). He argued further that the understanding of religion gathered by this method constituted the essence of what the Bible could provide to a systematic or dogmatic theologian.[3]

The effect of Gunkel's orientation to the psalms, which generally prevails in our own time, again colours how we hear Bonhoeffer's question. On the one hand, it underscores the antiquity of most of the psalms, in contrast to an earlier modern idea that these were products of the post-exilic period. On the other hand, it also underscores the vivid and richly human quality of the psalms read as ancient prayers of a long forgotten liturgy associated with the temple of Solomon and ancient Israelite worship. These insights are further collaborated by new archaeological discoveries of ancient Egyptian and Mesopotamian prayers which contain many features of a similar sort. So, in a strictly historical sense, Gunkel could argue that what these prayers best convey from the past is a register of what was characteristic of ancient spiritual life. More specifically, the typical and recurring elements in these prayers would unconsciously refer to the commonplace intellectual and spiritual assumptions of ancient Israel. This modern orientation to the psalms helps explain the formulation of Bonhoeffer's question because it directs our attention to the thoroughly human and ordinary character of these treasured prayers. How can such prayers so obviously directed to God be read as though they are God's address to us?

Finally, acceptance of these psalms *as prayers* confirms once again that most of these ancient traditions were not originally spoken or written down to be read *as scripture* at all. As noted before, in their oldest forms the psalms were historically not "biblical traditions" but, more accurately, "pre-biblical traditions." This recognition leads us to some additional questions parallel to Bonhoeffer's ques-

---

3. Hermann Gunkel, "Zeile und Methoden der Erfahrung des Alten Testament," pp. 11-29, *Reden und Aufsätze* (Göttingen: Vandenhoeck, 1913).

tion about the psalms. Why and how did the oldest prayers which once belonged to a hymn book of the first temple become part of a Jewish scripture? What alterations in the meaning or transformation in the semantic import of such pre-biblical traditions took place when they came to be read as part of a larger scripture? Only by a rigorous reassessment of how the prayers have been presented to us in this book of scripture can we begin to raise fully the modern theological question of how they can be read and heard as witnesses to God's word.

C. A RESPONSE TO MODERNITY:
LIBERALISM VERSUS LITERALISM

In the recent past the liberal modern response generally sought both to defend the validity of the aforementioned historical-critical insights into the psalms and to demonstrate their immediate religious or theological relevance. Biblical scholars tended to identify the most significant semantic level of these ancient prayers with the moment when they were first uttered. In this respect, liberal historical critics could claim to be doing nothing more than taking seriously the traditional affirmation of the church that the true literal sense of scripture is the same as the author's original intent. Of course, the trouble with this approach is that if the "author's intent" is identified with this modern historical view of authors, then a recovery of it will almost always be at the expense of the scriptural text itself. The "literal sense" in the eyes of the modern critic became less involved with the *scriptural* text and more based on the literary import of those pre-biblical texts or traditions that could be reconstructed. Of course, whenever critics associated their historical reconstructions with a desire to move closer to the actual moments of divine revelation in ancient Israelite history, their work could be accompanied by as much pious enthusiasm as one might find in the work of the so-called literalist opposition.

The conservative or fundamentalist response proves, in fact, to be no less modern or problematic in relation to traditional Christian interpretation. In my view, fundamentalism is a position advocating the right wing of modernism, old liberalism being on the left. One strength of fundamentalism was that it often correctly ascertained that liberal criticism threatened a basic protestant understanding of the scripture as the common object of Christian interpretation. However, this effort to defend the scripture presupposed the same modern historicism as that of the liberals. These so-called literalists tried to defend the validity of scripture by attempting to prove its historical accuracy. In the case of the psalms, they could argue that the attribution of the prayers to David was, in fact, historically accurate and that the titles that link some psalms to events in his life were written by editors during David's lifetime or shortly thereafter. While their arguments and expertise in ancient Near Eastern materials appropriately challenged some liberal critics, the fundamentalist position simply proved unconvincing as a whole and has lost credibility in all the major seminaries and universities.

I want to highlight two aspects of this problem created by the conservative position. First, the modern historical nature of this kind of interpretation put stress primarily on the historical and psychological dimensions of David's life. This approach tended, therefore, to create a single harmonized life of David. The significance of the psalms was thereby reduced to pious assessments of the historical David, reconstructed by conservative historical estimates. The results of this effort leave us with little more than a few psychological observations about David as a hero of faith.

A second problem for modern conservative interpretation concerns its inability to honor the church's classical affirmation of the literal sense of scripture. A distinction is commonly maintained within the tradition of the church between the grammatical sense of scripture and its literal sense. The grammatical sense, which included attention to details of historical etymology, preceded the reading of scripture's literal sense. By confusing the literal sense with the grammatical and historical features of the text, conservatives betray their own modernist impulse and distance themselves from earlier generations of interpreters. They lose sight of the larger context and scope of scripture. They become reactionary "historicists" rather than interpreters of the literal sense. The relation of the biblical text as a witness to its subject matter becomes ambiguous or lost entirely.

D. THE PSALMS AS SCRIPTURE

In the old debate between liberalism and literalism the form and function of the biblical text as a scripture within a religion has received surprisingly little attention. The reason for this blind spot is that the realism of a text had become associated almost entirely with the accuracy of its implied reference to past historical events. In more recent decades the modern philosophical self-doubt about metaphysics and, consequently, the challenge to the high role that modern history played in literary interpretation has opened the door to a fresh debate about the primary norms of reality and, therefore, realism. The modern fathers of suspicion — Freud, Nietzsche, and Marx — challenged the illusions inherent in a modern presentation of history. By the turn of the century, under the weight of these attacks, confidence in the "serious modern realism" typical of the nineteenth century Victorian novel (e.g., Macaulay, Thackeray, Dickens, and Brönte) was undermined by newer sociological, psychological, and economic theories.[4] These shifts in the general conception of realism point to suspicions, fostered in the succeeding decades up to the present moment, that we must surely now be "post-modern." The change in the intellectual climate of opinion regarding the relation between history and realism perhaps helps to explain why liberal historical critics have begun to re-evaluate more positively the role of editors in the formation of scripture, including their impact on the literary character of the scripture itself, and the relation of history both to whatever constitutes scriptural realism and to its possible claims of revelation. A revision in our understanding of the history of the interpretation of scripture was inevitable and the consequences for how we will apply the Bible to commentary and preaching are, at times, startling.

In the past two decades a reassessment of the book of Psalms as part of Jewish and later Christian scripture has taken place, principally among liberal historical critics. The implications of recent scholarly work offers a response to Bonhoeffer's question that goes well beyond either of the older liberal or literalist options.[5]

1. Psalm 2: From an Enthronement Liturgy to a Messianic Psalm

Since the form-critical investigations of Hermann Gunkel, scholars have usually regarded Psalm 2 as a "royal psalm." It does not open as a prayer, but has a liturgical character that might be explained by its derivation as part of a formal service in celebration of an Israelite

---

4. Cf. Frederic Harrison, *Studies in Early Victorian Literature* (London: Edward Arnold, 1901), pp. 13-15.

5. E.g., Walter Brueggemann, *The Creative Word: Canon as a Model of Christian Education* (Philadelphia: Fortress Press, 1982); Childs, *Introduction*, pp. 504-25 and his *Old Testament Theology in the Context of the Canon* (Philadelphia: Fortress Press, 1985), 204-221; Ronald Clements, *Old Testament Theology: A Fresh Approach* (Atlanta: John Knox, 1978), pp. 26-52; J. L. Mays, "The David of the Psalms" Interpretation 40 (1986) 143-55; Rendtorff, *The Old Testament*, pp. 246-50; and Gerald T. Sheppard, *Wisdom as a Hermeneutical Construct: A Study in the Sapientializing of the Old Testament* (BZAW, Vol. 151: Berlin: Walter de Gruyter, 1980), pp. 136-144.

king. Sigmund Mowinckel, Gunkel's student, developed this idea further in order to posit the occurrence of an elaborate royal enthronement festival analogous to such annual events in Egypt and Mesopotamia.[6] Despite the lack of explicit mention of such a festival in the Bible, this possibility still is among the most simple and probable historically. This hypothesis would also explain the occurrence and original usage of so many other royal psalms in the book of Psalms and elsewhere in the prophets. If we accept this historical possibility, or something similar, then various ambiguous elements within the psalm begin to assume a more explicit import. The fact that a royal figure is called "his anointed" (v. 2) reflects the ordinary circumstance that kings are "anointed" by a prophet or priest as a sign of God's sanctioning their sovereign appointment. In verse seven we have the statement by God, "you are my son, today I have begotten you." God's calling the king "my son" is common to language about kings in the Near East, as are exaggerated epithets about the king's power and wisdom (cf. Isa. 9:6). The statement, "Today I have begotten" might even be translated dynamically as "Today I have adopted you," the implication being that God annually re-establishes the king as his human surrogate in the leadership and administration of the people. The only obvious redactional addition to this psalm is the last line, "Blessed are all who take refuge in him." It is an independent formula that shifts the tone away from the logic that dominates the core of the psalm and it dangles as an afterthought at the end of a balanced statement regarding the kings of other nations and the consequences for the wicked in vv. 10-11. From this historical perspective the psalm becomes a source for reconstructing a "Davidic royal theology" that reflected for a long period of time the hope of ancient Israelite kings.

Without denying the value and continuing significance of such a historical reconstruction of the psalm, we should note that in this

6. Sigmund Mowinckel, *The Psalms in Israel's Worship* (New York: Abingdon Press, 1967) and his *He That Cometh*, trans. G. W. Anderson (New York: Abingdon Press, 1954).

treatment the psalm itself does not belong to scripture. It undoubtedly carries some authority — and might be called normative or even canonical for a moment in Israelite religion — but it belongs to the material of an ancient liturgy and not to a body of writings on a par with the Torah of Moses. Though God is quoted within the psalm and these authoritative words form part of a larger argument within it, the literary context is not yet that of scripture. Putting these matters more radically, we might say that in its original form it was intended only to be part of a special liturgical corpus and never part of a scripture of any religion.

This observation only heightens what is implied in Bonhoeffer's question: How can human words about God become God's word to us? Imagine how your congregation might react if next Sunday morning, after the reading of the biblical texts based on the lectionary, you explained, "I just could not find much in that biblical text, so I think I will preach this morning from one of my favorite hymns." Well, considering the state of preaching, the congregation would probably go along with you. If the next Sunday you said, "Once again, I could not find anything that spoke to me in the biblical passage, so if you will turn with me in your hymnals to page 142, I will preach on 'A Mighty Fortress is Our God,'" I suspect even your most devoted parishioner would begin to worry a little and openly rebel if it happened again. To a degree, I will argue that you are doing the same thing if you preach a sermon based only on such a historical reconstruction of Psalm 2 as a royal psalm which belongs to some ancient Israelite liturgy no longer mentioned explicitly in scripture.

We ought to realize, also, that when traditions that were originally pre-scriptural become part of a scripture they change their context and their semantic import. By analogy, we recognize that a word in a dictionary potentially has a field of meanings and that possibilities within that field are delimited by the specific use of the word in a given sentence and in a larger discourse. If I change the sentence I will change the delimited meaning of that word in either a subtle or radical way. So, we might ask more precisely what semantic transformation takes place when a royal psalm is taken up into the book of psalms as a book of scripture. Our best clues for an answer to this question can be found by paying attention to certain editorial features that by their nature betray a self-conscious effort to locate any particular text within a larger context of scripture.

In the scriptural context of Psalm 2, the older setting of a royal enthronement festival has been almost entirely lost. The rest of scripture never overtly identifies such a festival or retains any interest in how its liturgy made sense of these traditions. Despite the loss of its anchor in a particular liturgical event, the psalm fully retains some historical features from its original pre-history. The formulation, "You are my son, today I have begotten you" had, at the earliest historical level, always echoed a tradition of the promise of God to David by the prophet Nathan, a version of which is retained in the context of scripture in 2 Samuel 7. The psalm, now in its scriptural context, continues to assert that the Davidic king (the son of David) in Israel will be protected and sustained by God against all enemy nations. The Davidic king in ancient Israel is assured by God that if he will only "ask of me" (2:8), the nations, even the ends of the earth, will be the king's possession.

When we view Psalm 2 in this older historical relationship to the oracle of Nathan in 2 Samuel 7, we recognize that the promise given in Psalm 2, pertains, first of all, to David's immediate successor, his son Solomon. In the book of Psalms we, in fact, discover that two psalms, Psalms 72 and 127, are titled "A Psalm of Solomon." If we take the editors' work seriously, then we should try to see if either of these psalms plays upon Psalm 2 in the context of the book of Psalms. Psalm 72, regardless of our modern historical questions about its origins, is easily heard as Solomonic because of its internal references to his fame and honor among the nations who will reward the king with riches, even "gold of Sheba," v. 15 (remember the fame of Solomon among the nations, 1 Kgs. 3:29-34, 10:23-25, and the gold given him by the Queen of Sheba, 1 Kgs. 10:10). Psalm 72 is, also, marked editorially because it concludes the second of two collections of David psalms (cf. 3-41 and 51-71) in the first part of the book of Psalms — 72:20, "The prayers of David, the son of Jesse, are ended." In this psalm Solomon is presented as offering a prayer on behalf of the Davidic kings. By identifying himself as "the royal son" (v. 1) and by his summoning God to cause the kings of other nations to render him tribute and praise (vv. 8-11), Solomon appears to stand directly upon the promises stated in Psalm 2. He is presented as "asking" (2:8) God for help in just these matters. In other words, Psalm 72 in the context of the book of Psalms takes up the older historical import of Psalm 2 as a promise of God to sustain the ancient Israelite kings who belong to the dynasty of David.

Besides this association of Psalms 2 with pre-exilic Davidic kings, the psalm within the book of Psalms stands in the context of some other unusual "royal psalms" that suggest it came to be read as a messianic promise. Certainly the promise of Nathan to David in the psalm has as its intertext the deuteronomistic account of 2 Samuel 7 and, therefore, belongs to a larger scenario of biblical prophecy. The psalm has become one of several elements within that scenario, while losing its former role as a set piece within a particular liturgical tradition. In Psalm 89 we find again a recollection of the promise to David. Unlike the pre-exilic historical circumstances pertinent to the relationship of Psalm 2 to Psalm 72, Psalm 89 reflects a time when the monarchy has been destroyed by the Babylonian defeat of Judah in the first quarter of the sixth century. Just as in Psalm 2 we hear of the promise of God, "I have made a covenant with my chosen one, I have sworn to David my servant" (89:3) and that "with my holy oil I have anointed him" (89:20), so God answers, "I will not lie to David" (89:35), anticipating the sharp lamentation in the next part of the same psalm in which Israel in exile complains, "You have renounced the covenant with your servant; you have defiled his crown in the dust" (89:39). In this way, we see how Psalm 89 offers a fitting conclusion to the Davidic collections of lament psalms, playing directly off the promises of God to Nathan, reiterated at the outset of the book of Psalms by Psalm 2. Between Psalms 2 and 89 we are made to realize that a tremendous tension exists between the promises of God regarding his "anointed one" (2:2; 89:38, 51) and the hard fact that the Davidic monarchy has been destroyed (cf. similarly Psalm 132).[7]

The experience of national crisis during the exile is reflected in Psalm 89 and points us in a direction that far exceeds the pre-exilic hope of Israel. The context of these psalms indicates a radical reorientation of hope and a reinterpretation of the promise implicit in Nathan's original words to David in Psalm 2. The Hebrew word translated "the anointed" in Psalm 2 and 89 could, by the exilic period, be translated "the Messiah." According to an exilic Jewish hope in "the Messiah," we see how this promise could even seem to find some fulfillment in the appearance of the Persian king, Cyrus, who allowed Judah to return to the land and rebuild the temple. In Isa. 45:1 we read, "Thus says the Lord to his anointed/messiah, to Cyrus ... to subdue the nations before him." Cyrus is also addressed by God as "my shepherd" who "shall fulfill all my purpose" (Isa. 44:28). [8] There we can observe within the Old Testament itself how a hearing of Psalm 2 as messianic promise predates Christian interpretation. We can understand easily why the Jewish followers of Jesus could see him in these same terms. In the Gospel accounts we find the words of Psalm 2:7 — "you are my son, today I have begotten you" — which identify him as the Messiah at his baptism. Similarly, in Acts 4:23-28 the words of Psa. 2:1-2 are cited as confirmation of the prophecy about how the nations will relate to Jesus "his anointed" (in the Greek citation, lit. "his Christ"). In the context of scripture an

---

7.   Nahum Sarna, "Psalm 89: A Study of Inner Biblical Exegesis," pp. 29-46, in *Biblical and Other Studies*, ed. A. Altmann (Cambridge, 1963).

8.   Paul Hanson, *The Diversity of Scripture: A Theological Interpretation* (Philadelphia: Fortress Press, 1982), pp. 63-82.

older royal psalm has attained through its recontextualization and semantic transformation a capacity to be heard primarily as messianic promise. This biblical language about Jesus as "begotten" of God becomes basic to the early trinitarian doctrine in the second century A.D. The mystery implicit in the biblical language allowed the early Christians to confess things in common about Jesus without pretending to comprehend the full reality of what they could express in faith. In this way, a messianic interpretation of older prayers and liturgies is literally warranted by the context of Jewish and Christian scripture. For this reason, it is the confession of the church that Jesus Christ prays these prayers with us as the crucified messiah and takes our sufferings, as those expressed in the lamentations of these prayers, with him to the cross.

2. Psalms 1 and 2 as an Introduction to Psalms

Past critical scholarship portrayed the book of Psalms as a collection of independent prayers, arranged like a string of pearls on a necklace. Modern form criticism allowed us to identify most of the psalms according to their original form and function (hymns, laments, thanksgiving, wisdom, etc.). Admittedly these were not the same distinctions applied by the ancient Israelite scribes. Nevertheless, the form-critical study of the Psalms encouraged the impression that each psalm would have once existed as an isolated unit and that now these units appear in an almost random order within the book of Psalms. Though laments are predominant in the first half of the Psalms and hymns of praise in the last, there seemed little reason to draw any conclusion from that simple observation. However, as we shall show later, the use of titles and other features played a more significant role for the editors than these form-critical factors alone. In the case of Psalms 1 and 2 we have have assertions in pre-modern Jewish and Christian tradition (cf. Acts 13:33) that Psalm 2 could be cited as the "first" psalm. Rabbinic tradition explicitly states that the two psalms form a single introduction to the Psalms. A modern historical critical assessment of that possibility has begun only in the last twenty years.[9]

When we examine the first psalms for evidence of editorial features, we realize immediately that the titles for individual psalms do not begin until Psalm 3. Psalms 1 and 2 are juxtaposed without a title separating them. Though titles like that of Psalm 3, offering an historical setting for the psalm ("A Psalm of David when he fled from Absalom his son"), were probably composed by editors in the exilic period, their addition to psalms would have occurred in precisely the same period when the present book of Psalms was edited. So, the absence of titles for the first two psalms appears to be an intentional editorial device which set them off together prior to the titled psalms that follow.

Modern critics have commonly observed that the last line of Psalm 2 — "Blessed are all who take refuge in him" — also seems like an editorial addition since its style and content is not immediately related to the royal psalm that precedes it. If we consider Psalms 1 and 2 together as an introduction, we discover two remarkable effects of this addition at the end of Psalm 2. First, we observe that it has the same form as the first line of Psalm 1. The rabbis had traditionally commented on this fact by stating that the first psalm begins and ends with a "blessing." Second, using modern redaction criticism, we can see more clearly how the editors actually provided textual warrants for interpreting these two psalms together. The blessing in 2:11 serves as a transition between the message of the two introductory psalms and the prayers that follow them. Starting with Psalm 3ff., a whole series of individual lament psalms are found in which David is presented as taking refuge in God, for example, Psa. 3:1 "when he fled Absalom." Repeatedly within these psalms of

---

9. See, especially, Gerald Wilson, *The Editing of the Hebrew Psalter* (Atlanta: Scholars Press, 1985), pp. 138-228. On Psalms, see Sheppard, *Wisdom*, pp. 136-144.

lamentation, and often at the very beginning, we find the declaration of the psalmist: "I take refuge in you" or "you are my refuge" (e.g., 7:1; 11:1; 16:1; etc.). We might even speculate that the editors, recognizing these repetitions as a potential theme, may have derived the formulation at the end of Psalm 2 from Psa. 34:8b, "Blessed is the man who takes refuge in him." One consequence of this editorial marking of a theme throughout these psalms is that it encourages the reader to find here more than merely ancient prayers, but also to comprehend the variety of ways in which David took "refuge" in God. Editors further developed this theme for the first half of the book of Psalms by offering a negative example. The title to Psalm 52 presents that psalm as a prayer David offers soon after he was betrayed by Doeg the Edomite. According to the story in 1 Samuel 22, the implicit text behind this psalm title, Doeg was David's most unprincipled antagonist who killed the eighty-five priests who had hidden David from his enemy, Saul. In this psalm we read David's description of his enemy: "See the man who would not make God his refuge, but trusted in the abundance of his riches, and sought refuge in his wealth!" (v. 7). Whatever this psalm may once have signified historically, it now belongs to the tapestry of the Psalms as scripture, so that we read it in order to explore how we, like David, can find our "refuge" in God and in the Word of God rather than in our riches and wealth.

Our awareness of this editorial framework of "blessing" at the beginning and end of Psalms 1 and 2 encourages us to look more closely at how these two psalms might function together as an introduction to the book of Psalms. We have already seen how Psalm 2, perhaps once a royal psalm from an ancient Israelite enthronement festival, becomes a prophetic psalm of messianic hope in the context of the book of Psalms. Psalm 1 has been identified form-critically as containing elements of a torah psalm (celebrating or calling for obedience to the torah) and a wisdom psalm (offering advice like that found in Proverbs). Only verse 2 explicitly refers to the torah. If verse

2 is an editorial addition, then the original psalm would have been purely a wisdom psalm. The psalm "blesses" those who do not "walk in the counsel of the wicked" and concludes by contrasting the fate of the wise or righteous in verse 3 with that of the foolish or wicked in verses 4 and 5. Verse 6 summarizes the consequences of these two ways by means of a proverb. Even if verse 2 is an addition, which I think unlikely, the psalm as a whole now identifies the source of wisdom as "the torah of the Lord."[10]

At a minimum, we have in the present form of Psalm 1 the expression of a very common position regarding scripture in post-exilic Judaism (cf. Sir. 24; Bar. 3:9-4:4). The biblical presentation of a Mosaic torah was distinct from Solomonic wisdom books, which rarely mention the torah of Moses or other idiosyncratic historical convictions of Israel. Yet, as parts of scripture, torah and wisdom share in the same revelation of God. It became typical to assert each as a resource for the other: from wisdom we learn to better understand torah, from torah we learn to be wise. Scripture had established a difference between the idioms of the revealed torah and wisdom of God that only later scriptural interpretation could venture to reconcile. As noted before, in this post-biblical debate we find one of the primary resources for Jewish and Christian "ethics." Therefore, Psalm 1 has underscored the biblical subject matter of torah and wisdom, just as Psalm 2 highlights the idiom of prophecy. In other words, the two psalms together present the entire book as a resource for torah, prophecy and wisdom. The subject matter of the prayers in the Psalms is here declared to be the same as that of the rest of Jewish scripture!

We can ask further how the editors expect us to hear these two psalms together as dual psalms, with an interplay between them. The work of form critic Walter Zimmerli has helped us become aware that editors often put two psalms next to each other in order to

10. Cf. Leo Purdue, *Wisdom and Cult* (Missoula: Scholars Press, 1977), pp. 269-73.

indicate an intentional interplay between them.[11] The editors who
place them side by side may do so knowing that, when the two psalms
are read out loud together, the listeners will hear how each psalm
interprets the other, the whole being greater than the sum of its parts.
The editors have specifically indicated that Psalms 1 and 2 are to be
heard together by adding a blessing formula at the end of the second
psalm, a formula that recalls the beginning of the first psalm. When
we attempt to observe interplays between these two psalms we need
also to remember what distinguishes them from each other. The first
psalm is a torah and/or wisdom psalm while the second is topically
focused on the activity of nations and the king of Israel. The first
psalm carries a detached, didactic tone, rich in the balanced language
of generalizations, addressed to an attentive audience which, in this
case, includes you and me. The second psalm could be heard as the
voice of the king — v. 7, "I will tell of the decree of the Lord, He said
to me..." — again with a didactic force, including in its address both
us and perhaps the kings of other nations (v. 10) or, at least, if they
overhear this public admonition they will find themselves also within
its command. In brief, the first psalm offers a poetically abstract
generalization which the second psalm, then, illustrates in terms of
particular persons, the anointed king and the surrounding nations.
For the purpose of helping us see how the language of the two psalms
supports the interplays between them, I have translated the psalms,
putting a number of resonating elements in capital letters. Again we
might be able to hear these resonances far more easily than we can
see them when we read in silence.

> BLESSED IS THE MAN WHO
>   walks not in the COUNSEL of the wicked,
>   nor stands in the way of sinners,
>   nor SITS in the seat of SCOFFERS

---

11. Walter Zimmerli, "Zwillingspsalmen," pp. 105-11, in *Wort, Leid, und Gottespruch* [FS J. Ziegler]
(Würtzburg, 1972).

but his delight is in the law of the Lord,
   and HE MEDITATES ON THE LAW
     day and night.
He is like a tree planted by streams of water,
   one that yields its fruit in its season
     even its leaf does not wither
     in fact, in all that he does, he prospers.

Not so the wicked,
   rather, they are like chaff which the wind drives away,

Therefore,
   the wicked will not stand in judgment
     (even less so) sinners in the congregation of
     the righteous

For the Lord knows THE WAY of the righteous
   but THE WAY of the wicked WILL PERISH

Why do the nations conspire?
   (more so) why do THEY MEDITATE IN VAIN?
The kings of the earth collaborate,
   so they can plot together
     against the Lord and his anointed, saying,

       "Let us burst their bonds assunder,
       and cast their cords from us."

SITTING in heaven he LAUGHS,
   The Lord DERIDES them.

Then, he speaks to them in his wrath,
   terrifies them in his fury, saying,
     "I have set my king on Zion, my holy hill."

> Let me tell you about the decree of the Lord.
> The Lord himself said to me,
> > "You are my son,
> > I, this day, have begotten you.
> > Ask (for anything) from me
> > for I will give you the nations as your heritage
> > > even the ends of the earth as your possession.
> > You shall break them with a rod of iron,
> > > even dash them to pieces like a potter's vessel."
>
> Now, O kings, BE WISE
> > learn discipline O rulers of the earth.
> > Serve the Lord with fear, with trembling;
> > > kiss his feet [phrase uncertain]
>
> Lest he be angry, and you PERISH IN THE WAY,
> > for his wrath is quickly kindled.
>
> BLESSED ARE ALL WHO take refuge in him.

One of the most striking features to be noted is that Psalm 1 admonishes us to "meditate on the Torah day and night," while Psalm 2 states that the nations, by contrast, "meditate in vain ... against the Lord and his anointed." The same uncommon Hebrew verb, meaning "to meditate" or "to ponder," occurs in both of the psalms so that what we should do is set in opposition to what the nations presently do. Moreover, "the righteous" and "the wicked" of Psalm 1 correspond to "his anointed" and the attacking "nations" in Psalm 2. Likewise, as Psalm 1 ends on the somber note, "the way of the wicked will perish," so Psalm 2 concludes with an almost identical warning that the opposing nations will "perish in the way, for his wrath is quickly kindled." While Psalm 1 advises us not to "sit in the seat of scoffers," Psalm 2 tells us how God responds to the turmoil of the nations below, "He who sits in heaven laughs." As Psalm 1 specifies that the torah exists as a special source of wisdom

72

in Israel and that you and I should not "walk in the counsel of the wicked" so, in the following psalm, the nations are admonished, "Now, O kings, be wise." In this sense, a common thread is woven into both of the psalms. We have already observed that the editorial addition of the last line to Psalm 2 employs the same formula as found in the opening words of Psalm 1. Similarly, each of these blessings aims at "the man" or "all" in the sense of addressing any one of us.[12]

In sum, Psalms 1 and 2 prove to be an editorial introduction to the psalms that follow, and through a continuation of that role in later times, to the book as a whole. The central subject matter of Jewish scripture is affirmed at the outset (1:2), and the other idioms of revelation, wisdom and prophecy, are also fully expressed respectively in Psalms 1 and 2. Rather than telling us to read the prayers or to imitate them when we pray, Psalm 1 sets them forward first and foremost as aids in our meditation upon the torah. While we have in the psalms models of prayer, as the blessing at the end of Psalm 2 confirms, the primary role of these prayers as scripture is to teach us the torah. By implication, David's prayers have the capacity to be scripture because we are to read them not simply as prayers from his heart but as profound petitions to God based upon the Word of God. But in the hearing of scripture as such a witness both Jews and Christian hope that we may also find ourselves addressed by the subject matter itself, since the subject matter itself is not a dead object but the living Word.

12. A comment on the lack of inclusive language here ("man") in the biblical text of the first blessing: It is certain that this word could be translated "humanity" since its context does not require that its intent, despite its form, is gender specific. I think it remains important not to remove such offensive dimensions of the biblical witness even in a translation of the Bible. I would encourage some such changes in the liturgical use of scripture, however, since that context inherently invites the use of paraphrase. The fact that the wording of the witness of the text is disappointing should be no surprise. That is why we must preach the Bible for the Word of God and not simply confuse the two. For me *to preach* "blessed is the MAN" would only replicate literalistically the words of the text and indicate that I have failed to hear the Word of God which makes all such promises addressed to both women and men. Preaching should not simply repeat the Bible, but proclaim the Word of God.

Alongside this explicit emphasis upon the role of the psalms as a witness to the key idioms of scripture as a whole — torah, wisdom, and prophecy — we have seen that the messianic promise in 2:7 "You are my son, today I have begotten you" alludes specifically to the promise of Nathan to David in 2 Samuel 7. Hence, the principle of scripture interpreting scripture is presupposed in the nature of editorial formation of scripture itself. The force of this introduction to the psalms is to invite the reader to hear these prayers within the witness of the entire scripture. Finally, we should observe that the key idioms of biblical revelation affirmed by Psalms 1 and 2 are not without some formal correspondence to the psalms within the book itself. For example, the lengthy acrostic poem in Psalm 119 is composed to a great degree as an anthology of words and phrases drawn from other parts of scripture in celebration of the Torah. It has even been called by some scholars a "systematic theology" in miniature within the Psalms. Likewise, some psalms obviously correspond in their form more to wisdom literature (e.g., Psalm 37, 49) or to prophecy (e.g., Psalm 50) than to prayers. In any case, the literal sense of the book of Psalms as scripture is recognized only when we are able to hear it as a witness to this subject matter. This consideration of the Psalms as a whole book among other books of scripture leads us to examine how the form of it as a book might help us better appreciate its function as scripture.

3. A Bird's Eye View of the Book of Psalms

In pre-modern biblical interpretation Jewish and Christian tradition would sometimes describe the Bible as though it were a body with anatomical features or a foreign territory with its own unique topography. In the spirit of this older way of thinking about a text, we can employ modern redaction criticism in order to soar above the text and to envision it as a whole landscape composed of different traditions. One of the most obvious features in the organization of the book of psalms is the general rule that psalms of lamentation and complaint belong to the first half (3-89), while psalms of praise belong to the second (93-150).

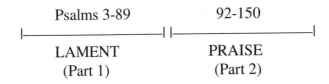

The Book of Psalms

Psalms 3-89   92-150
|————————————| |————————————|
LAMENT   PRAISE
(Part 1)   (Part 2)

Just as the prophetic books tend to organize oracles of judgment together into collections followed by oracles of promise, a similar pattern occurs in the psalms. This ordering of psalms in a book is also significant for later interpretation because it has sorted them out into topical categories of lament and praise with little or no effort to harmonize them and with almost no regard for their original liturgical functions. The original prayers can now be heard as a steady drumbeat, hammering away at the interpreter on the topics of lamentation and praise. This rhythm is achieved through the repetition of formal patterns in psalms belonging to the same type, through a redundancy of content, and through the recurrence of stock formulae which reappear suddenly as if they were musical refrains in the orchestration of a grand symphony.

The editors' juxtaposition of psalms of a similar type (mostly lamentation or praise) though with significant differences in content, establishes a contextual ambiguity. The hearers or readers of scripture must make discriminations that are not apparent in the text alone. This absence of harmony deepens the demand for interpretation of these prayers and even engenders an uninterpreted quality within the individual prayers that might not have been present when they were first composed. Whoever reads these prayers as scripture is led to ask a range of questions that cannot be answered solely by historical-critical investigations into their original life settings. Who are "the

enemies" that persecute the elect then and now? How do we pray
wisely so that what we claim about ourselves before God and others
is not really foolishness and self-deception? According to the torah
of God, when ought we to protest our innocence rather than confess
our sins? Are we thankful for the wrong things? On what promises
should we stand when we pray? In whose prayers might we be the
"enemies"? When are our prayers answered and how should we
acknowledge answered prayer before our believing sisters and
brothers?

A closer examination of the lament psalms (3-89) shows more
clearly how they belong to an edited composition. Without examin-
ing this organization in great detail we should notice at least that the
first part of the psalms is made essentially of two collections of David
psalms (3-41 and 51-71) and that the second collection has around it
a double bracket of Korah and Asaph psalms.

The first part of the Psalms

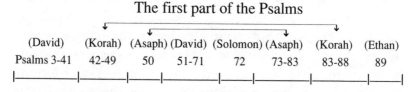

(David)	(Korah)	(Asaph)	(David)	(Solomon)	(Asaph)	(Korah)	(Ethan)
Psalms 3-41	42-49	50	51-71	72	73-83	83-88	89

In the positioning of the Korah and Asaph psalms we detect an
editorial device of using a double bracket or framework of similar
traditions around a central collection. It is an esoteric technique and
would probably only be easily recognized by other editors. Like
tailors who know what seam to look for in a well made suit, editors
of these texts could detect the use of aesthetic conventions that were
intended to be either subtle or overt. The same bracketing device
occurs in the composition of 2 Samuel 21-24 and in the arrangement
of judgment oracles around the testimony of Isaiah in Isa. 6:1-9:7.[13]

---

13. Cf. G.T. Sheppard, "The Anti-Assyrian Redaction and the Canonical Context of Isaiah 1-39,"
Journal of Biblical Literature 104/2 (1985) 196.

The important role assigned to Korah and Asaph in the Psalms demonstrates another key editorial feature by which other parts of scripture are related to the Psalms. 1 and 2 Samuel make no references to these persons in the portrayal of David's life. We find mention of Korah among the priests in the Mosaic Torah (in Numbers only), but none of Asaph. The account of David found in Chronicles goes beyond that of 1 and 2 Samuel by presenting him as the founder of the sanctuary worship services and the producer of hymns for that purpose (cf. 1 Chron. 6:31; 15:16-24; 16:4- 6,41). Within the Chronicler's account of specific worship events we find psalms from the book of Psalms quoted at length (cf. 1 Chron. 17). David appoints Korah and Asaph as liturgists at the temple and they are, with him, to compose hymns (cf. 1 Chron. 25:1-3). Another key element in this account is the repeated statement that David, Korah, and Asaph "prophesy" through this hymnology (cf. 1 Chron. 25:1-3; 2 Chron. 20:14; 2 Chron. 24:19). Hezekiah commands, for example, that psalms be sung "with the words of David and of Asaph the seer" (2 Chron. 29:30). This assertion that David psalms are forms of prophecy is corroborated editorially by the epilogue to 1 and 2 Samuel in David's "last words" in 2 Sam. 23:1, "The Spirit speaks by me, his word is upon my tongue." Little wonder that in rabbinic and Christian tradition it is common to speak of David as a prophet (e.g., Acts 2:29-30; Matt. 22:43; Lk. 12:36).[14] The implication for our understanding of the book of Psalms is that the editors regard it as a prophetic collection of hymns. That characterization immediately declares that the form and function of the Davidic Psalter invites an interpretation of the individual psalms as more than merely ancient Israel's prayers expressing a human word to God.

14. Cf. Nahum Sarna, "The Psalm Superscriptions and the Guilds," pp. 184ff., in *Studies in Jewish Religious and Intellectual History Presented to Alexander Altmann*, eds. S. Stein and R. Loewe (University: University of Alabama, 1979). For a careful overview of the distinctive ways David is presented in different traditions of scripture, see Alan M. Cooper, "The Life and Times of King David According to the Book of Psalms," pp. 117-131, in *The Poet and the Historian: Essays in Literary and Historical Biblical Criticism*, ed. Richard Elliott Friedman (Chico: Scholars Press, 1983).

We have already seen how the promise to the son of David in Psalm 2 corresponds to the prayer of Solomon, Psalm 72, placed at the end of the second David collection. The editorial note appended to the end of Psalm 72 states, "The prayers of David, the son of Jesse, are ended" (v. 20). Of course, in the second part of the Psalms (92-150), we find many more David psalms! Without entering into a debate about earlier levels in the editorial formation of the Psalms, we can, at a minimum, observe that the note at the end of Psalm 72 highlights the integrity of the first two collections of David psalms prior to the predominantly praise psalms that follow. The note reminds us that the association of David with the Psalms is a self-conscious one that underscores the nature of the tradition as a part of scripture in which the same David is described elsewhere.

In this overview of the Psalms as a whole we have not yet mentioned that the book is divided editorially into lesser books which, according to tradition, repeat the pattern of the five book Torah of Moses. Each of these five books ends with a brief doxology incorporating the expression "Amen" or "Amen and Amen" (cf. 41:13, 72:19, 89:52, 106:48). We notice how this pattern again conforms to the editorial distinctions we have been observing. Book 1 ends with the last David psalm in the first collection of David psalms; book 2 concludes with the Solomon psalm at the end of the second collection of David psalms, and book 3 finishes with Psalm 89 at the end of the double framework of Korah and Asaph psalms and recalls Psalm 2. This degree of organization should make us think that what follows Psalm 89 and stands between this section of primarily lamentation and praise hymns that follow (93ff.) is probably marked by the editors as a highly significant transition. So, when we turn to Psalms 90-91, what do we find?

It is surely no accident that Psalm 90 is the only psalm in the entire book of psalms attributed to "Moses, the man of God." Its position between the laments and praise makes even more sense when we find in it Moses doing what he does in the Torah, that is to say, interceding on behalf of the people: "Return, O Lord! How long? Have pity on your servant"(v. 13). The first verse uses a synonym for "refuge" and can be translated, "Lord you have been our refuge (dwelling place) in all generations" (cf. Dt. 33:27), recalling the theme of the prayers as a way to seek refuge in God which began in 2:12. Even as Psalm 1 referred to the Torah, Psalm 90 links all of the psalms to the prayer tradition of the Torah. This ordering of the psalms in the book of Psalms reinforces the correspondence in subject matter between the scriptural books associated with Moses and the book of Psalms as scripture associated with David.

The placement of Psalm 91, after the intercessory prayer of Moses in Psalm 90, is not arbitrary either. If the presentation of the wrath of God in Psalm 90 is severe enough to attract Martin Luther's use of it as a prime example of God's full judgment even against our hidden sins (90:7-8), Psalm 91 is news almost too good to be true. It explicitly takes up the language of "refuge" found in the first part of the psalms. Whoever "dwells in the shelter of the Most High" prays, "My refuge and my fortress, my God, in whom I trust" (v. 2). We are, then, assured that God "will deliver you" and "under his wings you will find refuge" (v. 4). We are told that "because you have made the Lord your refuge ... no evil will befall you"(v. 9-10). Little wonder that these promises came to be most readily associated with Jewish messianic hope in the post-exilic period. This way of hearing the text as scripture helps us understand better the pre-modern history of interpretation, including even the debate over the interpretation of the Bible between Jesus and Satan as presented in Matthew 4. Satan in the Temptations challenges Jesus to demonstrate his ability to fulfill the promises in Psalm 91 which assert, "He will give his angels charge of you ... On their hands they will bear you up, lest you strike your foot against a stone"(91:11-12, cf. Matt. 4:6). Just as Jesus has replied to the other temptations, he refuses to act messianically upon these promises and quotes instead from Deuteronomy 6:16, "You shall not tempt the Lord your God." In this "Battle for the Bible" in the wilderness both Satan and Jesus know how to read the Bible biblically. Satan tempts Jesus to confirm his identity by confirming literally and messianically the promises of Psalm 91, Jesus insists only on reasserting the common truths of the Torah that pertain to any Jewish believer. Those who are the most biblically literate will always find themselves, precisely because they have understood the scripture, in a valley of decision. What word of promise or what word of judgment pertains to my situation, here and now? In the case of the psalms, which of these prayers must I, at this moment, *not* pray?

4. David and the Psalms

A well established conclusion of modern critical scholarship is that many of the psalms could not have been written by the historical David. At the turn of the century, almost all of the psalms were thought to be post-exilic by liberal historical scholars who sought to investigate them using "source criticism" like that applied to the pentateuch. The advent of form criticism has led most scholars subsequently to the opposite conclusion, that most of the psalms may be pre-exilic at least in their origins. Some of them may actually derive from the historical David or be the work of hymnists (e.g., Korah and Asaph) under his supervision. Regardless, the short titles found appended to most of these psalms refer to David in a grammatically ambiguous manner. They consist of a preposition with a range of possible meanings — "of, for, to, with reference to, about, belonging to cycle of" — and the proper name, "David." They could be translated from Hebrew as "belonging to David," "of David," or perhaps even "about David" in the sense of "belonging to the cycle of traditions related to." Nonetheless, the role of these short titles as indicators of authorship in scripture becomes clear in the context of the longer historical titles linking prayers to certain events in the life of David (e.g., Psalms 3, 18, 34, 51, 52, 54, 56, 57, 59, 60, 63, 141). We doubt that these longer titles were original to the prayers because they have a fixed syntactical pattern suggestive of a learned editorial technique comparable to other related editorial devices. By studying the occurrence of similar editorial additions throughout the Old Testament we can roughly date when historical titles like these were appended to psalms. They probably belong to the exilic or post-exilic period about the time of 1 and 2 Chronicles, prior to the general shift in the use of such devices among editors that occurred by the time of the Septuagint. The "late" character of these titles is betrayed also by evidence of the editor's direct dependence on the stories about David that we have in 1 and 2 Samuel. From a modern historical perspective they can be regarded as secondary efforts, derived long after the time of David, to exploit points of correspondence between stories about him and prayers that may or may not have derived from him.[15]

A liberal response that devalues the psalm titles on the basis of this historical information appears in the modern translations. For example, "The New English Bible" simply eliminates all of the titles to the psalms. The "Today's English Version," known popularly as the "Good News Bible," puts all of the titles in footnotes at the bottom of the page and has inserted in their place modern thematic titles: for Psalm 3, "Morning Prayer for Help." The effect of this modification of the biblical text is to minimize the association of the Psalms with David and to undo the logic of the collection itself so that the psalms become a string of isolated units of prayer, each perhaps offering its own little thematic contribution. Modern liberal commentaries often ignore the possibility that the titles may offer help in the understanding of the psalms themselves. Conservative evangelicals or fundamentalists may try to defend on scholarly grounds the historical value of the titles, but with little hope of ever convincing most of their modern biblical colleagues. Even more significantly, a historically conservative use of these titles differs also from that which we find earlier in the history of biblical interpretation. In conformity to a modern historicist notion about how these texts have meaning, conservatives find in these titles a window into the psychology of the

---

15. Brevard S. Childs, "Psalm Titles and Midrashic Exegesis," *Journal of Semitic Studies* 16 (1971) 137-50.

historical David who lies outside of scripture as a subject for our pious assessment. Why the prayer life of the historical David is of great theological significance for Christians belongs to a theological problem of its own and we are back to Bonhoeffer's question in a modified form: How can the words in these prayers, belonging in all of their particularity to the historical David, relate to my own prayers, much less be God's word to me? In other words, if the subject matter of these prayers is the historical David's spirituality, then it still remains unclear how that information pertains to my knowledge of the revealed torah, promise, and wisdom of God, much less the Gospel of Jesus Christ.

I want to consider what is involved in moving beyond both a liberal reading that ignores these titles as "late" or "non-genuine" and a modern conservative reading that uses the titles of the psalms as merely psycho-historical references to David. First, any liberal effort to remove the psalm titles violates its own principles if many other parts of the psalms are not removed at the same time. Once the process of removing late material from the psalms begins it should not be arbitrary but aimed at some theoretical level of literary composition so that we finally have before us a text as it once existed rather than an entirely hypothetical text. The most basic question remains, "What text do you want?" If we want the original prayers of David, then we must atomize the book of Psalms in order to recover them. The "original" prayers were scriptures to no one, so if we want to see how they appear as scripture we must find a text in which they have attained their form and function as parts of scripture. In other words, when we, on the basis of modern historical criticism, reconstruct the original prayers of David from scripture we almost invariably de-scripturalize the biblical traditions in the course of doing so and what we recover will be in a pre-scriptural (or pre-biblical) form. The question of *how* these pre-biblical, often oral, prayers became written scripture can be answered only by showing how their form and function has been changed.

As a second consideration, the content of these titles suggests that they derive from a time when the editors of the Bible had before their eyes both a book of Psalms and the same canonical stories of David as we find in 1 and 2 Samuel. The titles are, consequently, a good example of "inner-biblical" interpretation, that is to say, interpretations found in scripture that relate various parts to each other. The effect of the titles is to draw a few representative lines from the accepted stories about David to the psalms of David, lines that apparently existed before as implicit possibilities integral to the very nature of a scripture. These editorial contributions presuppose that the stories about David and the body of the Psalms are now being viewed together as part of the same scripture. Though these traditions may or may not have been related prior to their mutual incorporation into scripture, they now belong to a common written text. Hence, the titles are not a late intrusion into scripture, but are constitutive of a scripture that is itself comprised of traditions not originally considered scriptural in this same sense at all. Expressed in a different way, the historical psalm titles are less an innovation than a response to the new force these traditions exerted as part of a scripture on the reading public. These collections of ancient traditions are now heard collectively as bearing witness to one and the same religious reality and, in the reception of them in this way, certain points of correspondence within the diversity of that witness become obvious and are occasionally made explicit by the editors.

Third, we have already seen how Psalms 1 and 2 provide an introduction to the book of Psalms. There we find the presupposition that the subject matter of the psalms is the torah, prophecy, and wisdom revealed by God, corresponding to what is already familiar elsewhere in scripture. By implication, the subject matter of these psalms, as prayers transformed into a part of scripture, is *not* the spirituality of the historical David. The aim of the book is not to give us insight into the psychology of the historical David; its purpose is not to satisfy our modern desire to imagine this king as an archetypal "hero" who faithfully turns to God when he is under stress.

Nevertheless, the editors have endeavored to increase, rather than to diminish, David's significance in the book. From a modern critical perspective, we might say that they have, in some cases, actually historicized once independent, typical instances of prayer by assigning them to specific moments in the life of David. This same tendency also underlies a repetition of the same psalm in Psalm 18 and in 2 Samuel 22. The psalm in 2 Samuel belongs to a carefully constructed conclusion and interpretation of the life of David at the end of 1 and 2 Samuel. David has become firmly associated with the whole book of Psalms. Despite the presence of many psalms assigned to other figures before and after his time, the presentation of David within the book and elsewhere in scripture provides the key sign of the book's coherence, as well as the context of its interpretation as a part of a larger scripture. We begin to realize that the pre-scriptural hymns can be heard scripturally only when they are heard in just this association with David.

If we are to go beyond liberalism and literalism, we must ask how we, as modern interpreters, can interpret scripture without reducing it either to its etymology of pre-scriptural hymns in ancient Israel or to a historical reconstruction of the life of David. Either move, whether conservative or liberal, forfeits with equal success the context and the subject matter of scripture. Conversely, I propose that the cumulative presentation of David within scripture serves us less well as a reference to ancient history than as a realistic depiction of the human witness to divine revelation, according to pre-modern and popular norms of history. Within scripture itself, we find traditions that represent different and changing concepts of "history." From this perspective, differing conceptions of history within the pre-history of the biblical traditions belong to the etymology of scripture rather than to the subject matter of scripture itself. Without any doubt, our modern knowledge of history should help us to recognize the historical complexity of scripture and in *ad hoc* ways it will help us to clarify vaguenesses and to heighten realism in the scriptural presentation of persons and events. Even a trip to modern Israel can cause the Bible to come alive for similar reasons, partly because the realism in the presentation of persons and events in scripture is not identical with the"realism" implicit in a modern account of ancient history. This matter is similar to the problem of how scientific modern conceptions of reality relate to theological discourse about reality. Langdon Gilkey confronted this issue in the debates between evolutionists and creationists. He reminds us that each discipline, science and theology, operates with a different "mode of understanding" and that discourse from one cannot uncritically be imported over into the discourse of the other.[16] Accordingly, the "realism" of the biblical presentation corresponds only to a mode of understanding congruent to the nature of scripture and its religious interpretation. Biblical realism should never be expected to satisfy exactly the same norms of "realism" belonging to the mode of understanding congruent to a modern conception of history, despite the family resemblance here and there between each perception of what is realistic.

The realistic presentation of David in 2 Samuel resembles modern historical realism so much that Gerhard von Rad saw in these narratives the beginning of historical writing.[17] The high historical quality of these narratives has persuaded modern biblical scholars to mine from them as much modern historical information as possible, Still, when a modern historical reconstruction, no matter how appreciative it may be of the accuracy of the biblical account, employs the biblical text as only one among many extra-biblical sources of reference to the past, then the context of scripture itself is abandoned. In a similar way, conservative or fundamentalist scholars just as

16. Landgon Gilkey, *Creationism on Trial: Evolution and God at Little Rock* (Minneapolis: Winston Press, 1985), pp. 212-218.

17. Gerhard von Rad, *Old Testament Theology*, (New York: Harper & Row, 1962), Vol. 1, pp. 316-18.

often unintentionally distort the biblical text in order to employ it apologetically to defend a modern conservative view of the biblical pre-history. An understanding of the Bible's own terms of realistic presentation requires a very different approach. I will briefly mention three implications of David's role in the Psalms' realistic depiction of him.

1. The association of the Psalms with a particular person, David, indicates that there is some literary coherence to this collection. The assignment to David signifies that the psalms can be read as though they belong together and as though each psalm pertains to its subject matter in a similar way. Just as the traditions that comprise the pentateuch can be read as the books of Moses and the primary witness to the Torah, so the books of Solomon can be read as a primary source of wisdom. Similarly, the assignment of names to individual prophetic collections divides the mass of prophetic traditions in ancient Israel into little unities, what we have come to call "books," with distinctive sets of resonances and innerplays within each. This same feature is sufficiently established for David and the Psalms, despite the obvious fact that many psalms are assigned to people other than David and even to later figures, such as Solomon. The very expression, "the Psalms of David" indicates an act of interpretation warranted by this association and it engenders the possibility that this literature, as diverse as it may be, functions as a separate literary entity in relation to other books of the Bible. The identity of David is also significant because he plays a role elsewhere in scripture as the person most intimately involved with the organization of Israel's worship. In other parts of the Bible David is depicted as a person who is is obedient to the law, endowed with prophetic powers, and skilled as a wise king. This background underlies all later messianic hope that longs for a son of David who would fulfill all the major offices of scriptural witness — prophet, priest, king, and sage — and, concomitantly, master all the subject matter of revelation. Accordingly, David is portrayed as the great synthesizer of the truths of

scripture. Beyond offering us models of prayers, the book of Psalms — as the introduction of Psalms 1 and 2 make clear — present these prayers as objects of meditation and study, and as inner-biblical commentary on the torah, prophecy, and wisdom.

2. By their association with a particular person, David, the actual words of the book are not simply identical with the Word of God and the subject matter of scripture. Because the words of these psalms are, on one level, David's words, the text itself is never allowed to float free from its constitution as a human witness to divine revelation. This literary characteristic holds this text of psalms firmly to the earth within the larger intertext of scripture which presents David as both a "man after God's own heart" and as a repentant sinner. This aspect of the scripture ensures reception of it as a fully human word, undercutting all docetic positions regarding the nature of scripture. At most, Jewish and Christian believers can seek to articulate a doctrine of "inspiration" that builds on the identification of David as a prophet, but must incorporate into this presentation the full humanity of David. The problem of the "inspiration" of scripture cannot be treated adequately within the limits of these essays, but we might at least note in passing that any modern discussion of the "inspiration" of the person of David needs to be fully aware of the dialectical relationship between what can be said about David through modern historical investigations and how the Bible presents the David of history. The reduction of the biblical David to a modern portrait of the historical David, whether conservative or liberal, frames the question of inspiration from a position outside of scripture and is alien to the logic of the scripture's own form and function.

3. As mentioned before, the titles of some psalms identify them with particular events in the life of David. A few psalms even mention David and his fate within the prayer itself (cf. 78:67-72; 89; 132). Within the larger framework of scripture the David of the Psalms is the same as the David in the narratives and these two resources collaborate in our interpretation. The presentation of

David is an integral part of the syntax that holds these different books
of scripture together. If we examine the titled psalms carefully in the
light of the narratives in 1 and 2 Samuel, we realize that the titles are
not arbitrary additions to the psalms. Key words or phrases between
the psalms and their relevant narratives allow them to be heard
together in a strong, evocative manner. For example, Psalm 3 by its
title presupposes that we know the details about how Absalom,
David's son, attempted to seize the throne from his father and how
David fled from his palace in the dead of night. Suddenly. the realism
of the words of the psalm gains keen vividness and refinement. When
in Psa. 3:5 he says, "I lie down and sleep, I wake up for the Lord
sustains me," we recall that David had to risk camping out at night
before he could cross the Jordan River to take sanctuary in a foreign
nation. Absalom's failure to follow the advice of Ahithophel to
pursue his father demonstrates God's intervention on David's behalf
(cf. 2 Sam. 17:14). The descriptions in the prayer of "the tens of
thousands" (Psa 3:6) set against David corresponds well to the army
Ahithophel wanted to send immediately in pursuit of David (2 Sam.
17:1). Even if, from a modern perspective, the original psalm behind
Psalm 3 had little to do with David and nothing to do with this
historical event in David's life, it does now in the context of its role
as scripture. We cannot make the Bible a better scripture by reconstructing earlier levels of its text and context. Only by honoring the
logic of scripture itself can we understand how scripture interprets
scripture so that the psalms depict the inner life of David, alongside
the rendering of David as a public figure in the other biblical books.
It is a strength of scripture that it can offer just this sort of depiction
of reality, one that lies beyond the ordinary confidence and competence of modern historical inquiry, liberal or conservative. This
characteristic in the context of Christian scripture accounts for the
need, in my view, of a "literal" type of biblical interpretation which
is underestimated or devalued by both contemporary liberal and so-
called literalists alike.

5. Psalm 51 as an Illustration

As I have argued throughout these presentations, the choices between liberalism and literalism represent for me false options within
late modernity. A liberal approach to the Psalms tends to be associated with the modern historical reconstruction of oral traditions of
ancient prayer. Conversely, a conservative historical approach may
make the assumption that the present form of the biblical text refers
accurately to past persons and events in a way that is congenial to how
modern historians construe the historical past. The "liberal" easily
becomes pre-occupied with the social and historical etymology of the
biblical text, inspired by the richness of the Bible's pre-history. The
so-called "literalist" confuses the realism of the text itself with a
conservative modern account of history, then tries to defend its
veracity by appeals to ancient facts about persons, places, and things.
In both cases the realism constituitive of scripture is lost, either to the
left or right wing of modern historicism.

This problem can be illustrated concretely by considering Psalm
51. The historical title associates this psalm with a particular event in
the life of David: "A psalm of David when Nathan the prophet came
to him, after he had gone to Bathsheba." From a modern historical
perspective, we would argue that this statement was probably added
to the psalms in the post-exilic period. The earliest level of the
original prayer is preserved only in vv. 1-17; vv. 18-19 appear to be
another editorial addition that reflects concern for God to "rebuild the
walls of Jerusalem" (v.18b) and to reinstitute sacrifices at the new
temple which was built under Ezra and Nehemiah (v. 19). Additions
like these last two verses occur in several other psalms and probably
reflect a widespread "up-dating" of earlier prayers in terms of the later
hope during the period of exile after the destruction of the temple in
Jerusalem and before the return to the land. Obviously, these words
may sound strange coming from the mouth of David who had just
built some of the walls of Jerusalem and now prays for God to
"rebuild" them.

The earliest portion of this prayer, 51:1-17, is, in form-critical terms, a penitential prayer of an individual. It begins with an initial plea (vv. 1-2), confesses sin (vv.3-6), offers a petition (vv. 7-12), and concludes with the customary vow (vv. 13-15). The note about right sacrifices (vv. 16-17) may have belonged to this petition or it could also be a later addition on the theme of sacrifice. The vow would have been the expected way to conclude a penitential lament. This historically non-specific prayer once probably served as a reusable vehicle of confession that could be employed by anyone who found it appropriate. It provided the worshipper with a competent oral petition to God for any very serious error or crime. Its artistic precision and proper form made it an eloquent counterpart to the unblemished sacrifice that one might bring to the occasion of seeking divine redemption while confessing a terrible sin. The reference to broken bones in v. 8 might suggest an illness or physical injury. The criticism of sacrificies in vv. 16-17 may be a warning about the abuse of sacrifices like that we find in both the prophetic and priestly traditions (cf. Amos 5:21-24 and Psalm 15). [18] In its pre-biblical form, the core tradition of Psalm 51 has its own integrity, though with no pretention of being a text of "scripture" for any known religion.

The exilic addition to this prayer in vv. 18-19 plays upon the preceding verses, and raises the possibility of "right" sacrifices when Jerusalem once more becomes the center of worship. The addition of the title, perhaps still later, occurred when editors sought to make some explicit connections between a "Davidic" Psalter and the depictions of David found in the prophetic books of 1-2 Samuel. Implicit in this latest activity is the assumption that the editors would have had both texts before them and accorded both a similar scriptural status. Rather than viewing these editorial contributions as moments of pious deception, it is more reasonable to assume that editors sought to develop what would have been obvious to them but might have

18. Erhard S. Gerstenberger, *Psalms*, Vol. 1 (Grand Rapids: Eerdmans, 1988), pp. 211-15.

been in danger of being overlooked by others. After all, a highly competent reader of all of these scriptural texts together would be aware that this psalm has the unusual line, "Against thee, thee only, have I sinned" which corresponds to the equally rare confession of David, "I have sinned against the Lord" (2 Sam 12:13).

These historical-critical observations about the psalm demonstrate that we can break it apart and find within it earlier and later traditions. There is nothing illegitimate about reconstructing any of the pre-biblical prayers concealed within this psalm, and a modern historian must work this way. Whatever text is read, for whatever purpose, it should benefit from historical knowledge about what I would call the grammar and etymology of the biblical text. Historical criticism ought to help us clarify vaguenesses and heighten the realism of whatever text we want to interpret. My goal is not to devalue historical criticism in any way, but to ask what constitutes the scriptural character of the psalms, and, therefore, how I can read them as both the words of men and women to God and as God's Word to me.

Read as a part of scripture, the title of Psalm 51 helps us as readers because it refracts how we can understand this text as a part of scripture. The title of the psalm does not satisfy our desire to understand so much as it establishes the arena in which a profound understanding may take place. It highlights only one particular dimension within the poly-valency of a text that could, otherwise, be heard and read merely as a simple prayer to God. The addition of the title clearly places the psalm at a particular point within the cummulative depiction throughout the Bible of the figure of David. The psalm in this context discloses David's full response to God under the circumstance of his most flagrant and public breaking of the law of God.

Admittedly, the last two verses of this psalm create a problem for the very careful reader who associates these words with the life of

David. If these words are regarded as an expression of hope from the
exilic period that the walls David had built would be reestablished,
then how could David in his own day have uttered them in prayer?
This dilemma was observed in the pre-modern period and a common
solution was to recall David's role as a prophet. In that role, David
could appear to be speaking prophetically of a future time when the
walls will have fallen. On behalf of future Israel in exile, David
implores God for their repair. Our modern knowledge of historical
criticism has sharpened this anachronism within the psalm by anchor-
ing the origins of each part of the psalm in two different periods and
by detaching the historical David from both of them. We are now
aware that if we are to interpret scripture at all, we must be able to
sustain the text within its scriptural context and, then, see if we can
still recognize there the realistic features that pertain to its scriptural
function as a human witness to God's revelation. How the text can be
sustained as a scriptural text — within the common hearing and
effective vision of its interpreters — is directly affected by our special
grammatical and etymological knowledge of the text's pre-history.
Our task will necessarily be different to some degree than that of
earlier generations because our understanding of the matters has
changed. This interpretation cannot preclude, at the outset, that the
scriptural context might be sustained at places only in the barest
literary fashion with little or no support from a modern knowledge of
history. What may be a case of blatant anachronism from the vantage
point of a modern historian may prove to play an integral role in the
depictive realism of a text. A biblical text may result from a composite
of entirely unrelated sub-texts which are juxtaposed in a way that
serves a new ingenious purpose, or constitutes a profound ambiguity,
or leaves the reader with a flat contradiction. Our knowledge of
historical criticism ought to help us in the recognition of these
differences. We might protest — a protest brash enough to be modern
— that we could have written a better scripture, if God had just had
the patience to wait for our more historically informed generation to
be the bearers of revelation. Otherwise, we must join all the preceding

who, no less than we today, have found the attempt to read the scripture scripturally a foretaste of heaven at times and at other times profoundly unrewarding.

Turning to the specific case of Psa 51:18-19 and our present investigation of its literal sense, we can make the following observations. When I sustain the context of scripture, I notice that the petition form of the discourse, as shown in the imperatives — "do good to Zion" and "rebuild the walls" — continues the same form of discourse found before in the body of the psalm, e.g., "have mercy on me" (v. 1) and "open my lips so that my mouth might give you praise" (v. 12). By this device the same voice is maintained within the entire psalm. As in the similar case of the presentation of the voice of Isaiah with the two parts of the book of Isaiah (chapters 1-39 and 40-66), a shift has taken place in tone and in content. Now David is presented as no longer concerned only with his own person, but with Zion and the walls of Jerusalem. What links the earlier preoccupation with his own person to this shift of concern to Jerusalem is a common thread within the petition that God should "wash," cleanse," "create," "restore," "deliver," and, here in v. 18, "do good to" and "rebuild." Moreover, while David had known earlier that God wanted from him a "broken spirit" and a "contrite heart" instead of a sacrificial offering, the last verse portrays David as longing for a time when "right sacrifices" will be offered once more in Jerusalem. Within the context of this specific, titled psalm and the scriptural intertext of 1 and 2 Samuel we can detect other realistic resonances with the last two verses of the psalm. David's act of adultery and his killing of Uriah, the husband of Bathsheba, is a turning point in the story of David. Nathan's ominous words of judgment — "the sword will never depart from your house because you have despised me and have taken the wife of Uriah the Hittite to be your wife" (2 Sam 12:13) — tinges every subsequent act of David and his household. The concluding retrospective commentary on David's life in 2 Samuel 21-24 reminds us of it again by naming "Uriah the Hittite" (2 Sam 23:39) at the very end of the second of two lists of "mighty men" who fought bravely for David in the war against the Philistines (2 Sam 21:15-22 and 24:8-39). Alongside its personal consequences for David, "the sword" that swung against the house of David also held direct implications for the future of Jerusalem.

So, David's confession of his sin and his pleading for "a new and right spirit" and a return of "joy" is presented here accompanied by his knowledge that the city walls he so carefully constructed are equally in shambles, as is his personal life. In a sound prophetic sense typical of scripture, the walls are as good as fallen and, therefore, David actually stands already in the rubble of the glorious city he himself has built. All that David can do is plead with God, as did later exilic Israel in Psalm 89, that God will restore what has been destroyed. The historical anachronism, from a modern critical perspective, does not function as an anachronism in the realistic depiction of scripture because David, in fact, thanks to the prophecy of Nathan, knows about events that have for him and at that very moment, occurred, so to speak, ahead of time. The words of David do not pretend to predict the future as much as they interpret a whole spectrum of ordinary events from an extraordinary prophetic perspective, one outside of the perogative of a modern historian. In the broken heart of David, we see the breached walls of Jerusalem during the time of the Judean exile.

What must be illuminated by our use of modern historical knowledge is the text itself as a human witness rather than speculation about the historical David. Historical criticism has performed a necessary heuristic function as a caution against any tendency toward historical harmonizing of the ancient traditions that are retained in the scriptural texts. In this example, I have also tried to avoid a literalistic psychologizing of David without denying the illuminating advantage of some *ad hoc* psychological dimensions in the realistic depiction of David. The desperation expressed in the words of repentance in the psalm carry a certain ideosyncratic weight and emotive force when they are heard specifically in the context of details about David's life in 1 and 2 Samuel. We can and should recognize something true about David and ourselves in similar situations. This work of interpreting the psalms pushes us to hear in the depictive realism of the text a trustworthy testimony to God's revelation about human nature, what might be called technically, theological anthropology. We are encouraged by Psalm 1 and 2 to be further attentive to the biblical idioms which, in the language of faith, articulate its subject matter. We read this psalm as a way to meditate upon the law of God and our own situation of obedience or disobedience. We examine the prayer as a source of wisdom so that we might know how to pray under such circumstances and so that we might recall by proverb and parable the logic of our wise and foolish acts. As Jews and Christians, we learn once more how to rely on God's promises and to fear the judgment of God who stands on the side of justice.

6. A Concluding Theological Postscript

Our treatment of the Psalms began with Bonhoeffer's question. We have ventured only a partial answer to it. The larger issue, how human words to God become God's Word to us, raises many theological problems we have not even considered. What I have suggested is that we are in a new situation in biblical studies that might allow us to respond to Bonhoeffer's question from a fresh perspective. We recognize through historical criticism that many, if not most, traditions that have been taken up into scripture were not originally intended to be scripture. By maintaining a sensitivity to the role of scripture in Judaism and Christianity, we can begin to describe how the context and intertext of scripture reflects a transformation of mere human words into a biblical witness to divine revelation. In my view, biblical interpretation by both liberals and literalists has become confused about the nature of scripture and, therefore, remains uncertain about how scripture itself relates to the subject matter of faith. It is difficult to hope for constructive arguments about the theological implications of scripture for contemporary problems if we disagree, in the first place, on the most basic issues of how to read the Bible biblically.

One of the most significant consequences of asking this basic question about the form and function of scripture is that it sheds light on how we perceive boundaries and ambiguities in our interpretation of scripture. One example is that the psalms by their own recurring structure and formulaic language reflect some norms of linguistic competence and essential characteristics of articulate prayer. Within these boundaries Christians may be surprised at how forcefully we are free to challange and complain to God about our suffering. These complaints may even include reproachful questions as found in Psalm 22 and Jesus' words on the cross, "My God, my God, why have you forsaken me." A substantial ambiguity exists in how we might express our own lamentations to God: we can either protest our innocence (e.g., Psa. 26:1-12) or we can confess our sins (e.g., 41:4-13). So, deciding whether our suffering is a consequence of our own foolishness or entirely unjust, perhaps due to the prejudice of others, becomes a major issue in how we pray; and if we pray the wrong way we exhibit bad faith and perpetuate an illusion. Gentle and kind people more concerned with order than justice may tell us to confess sin when we should protest innocence and we should realize at the same time that they are perhaps our enemies. It is just as much a sign of bad faith to confess sin when we should protest innocence as it is to claim innocence when we should admit our sin. How we decide these matters is obviously more than academic. How we pray, in the language of faith, circumscribes our hope in God and names the reality of life around us.

Returning to Bonhoeffer's profound question with which we began this study, we can now summarize some of our responses to it. First, the book of Psalms does not preserve these prayers as isolated moments of an antique spirituality of ancient Israel. These prayers have already been transformed semantically by the new role they have come to play within scripture. The existence of scripture necessarily presupposes the existence of a community of faith which discerns the providence of God in the processes by which some traditions belong to scripture and others do not. We observe, secondly, that the book of Psalms is organized as the prayers of David and belongs, accordingly, within a specific intertext of scripture. The realistic presentation of David throughout the Bible and particularly in the book of Psalms constitutes an integral element in the syntax of scripture, guiding us in our reading of these ancient traditions as scripture. In this respect, the attribution of prophetic authority to David, as well as to Korah and Asaph, further certifies the human voices of these texts as witnesses to God's revelation.

Thirdly, the introduction of Psalms 1 and 2 confirms that the psalms are not merely prayers to God but give instruction in the Word of God. The distinctive formal character of the psalms and the orchestration of formulae within them convey also that they are learned prayers rather than prayers from the heart. We, therefore, discover in them an invitation to offer disciplined prayer even when our hearts are empty, precisely because our hope lies not in the poverty of our imagination but in the richness of the Word of God. Finally, as Bonhoeffer so well recognized, the new claim of Christianity is that Jesus Christ, as the Messiah, also prays these prayers with us. Since these prayers within Christian scripture point to the same Word of God more fully revealed in the New Testament, they bear witness for Christians to the torah, prophecy, and wisdom of God which find fulfillment in the Gospel of Jesus Christ. For this reason, we read the Psalms in the context of Christian scripture both to treasure our common inheritance of the Word of God with Judaism and to comprehend the Gospel.

I am less troubled about the present conflict within the United Church than I am about the crisis in our churches over how to preach and to teach the Bible as a guide to a life of faith. The theological goal of biblical study is, of course, not to know the Bible itself, but to know

97

God. The aim is to find and to be found by Jesus Christ, whom we discern in the power of the Holy Spirit as the way, the truth, and the life. The Bible as scripture should provide the arena in which fruitful, public controversy on such matters can take place. Any other battle over the Bible, conducted in any other arena will be only a conflict over who will be better prepared to give a dead letter a proper burial.

III

Solomic Wisdom
Literature: How Should
We Answer the
Riddles of the
Queen of Sheba?

A. INTRODUCTION

The depiction in 1 Kings 10 of the visit by the Queen of Sheba to test Solomon's wisdom should be set against the background of Israel's history of slavery in Egypt a few generations before. Sheba was a fiercely independent country isolated in southern Arabia, approximately where eastern Yemen is today. It controlled trade routes from Africa to the north and west, as well as sea routes. In Isa. 45:14 it is associated with "the wealth of Egypt and the merchandise of Ethiopia." Sheba became well-known for its trade in spices, precious stones, and gold (cf. Isa. 60:6; Jer. 6:20; Ezek. 27:22). Solomon would have commercial reasons to have good rapport with this people who controlled a gateway city to the African northeast, including especially Egypt. The Sabeans of Sheba were prominent traders in the ancient Near East, and, in modern terms, sources of news and referees of international opinion. It is in this latter role, that Sheba, so closely linked in its trade to Egypt, plays a special role in the attestation of Solomon's wisdom. Here we should remember how Israel would appear to the Sabeans. The conventional Israelite credo recalls, "A wandering Aramean was my father, and he went down to Egypt ... and the Egyptians treated us harshly and afflicted us ... but the Lord brought us out of Egypt with a mighty hand ... and brought us to this place and to this land..." (Dt. 26:5-8). So, there is considerable irony in this story about Israel, whose founding mothers and fathers had been slaves in Egypt. Only a few generations later, this state of Israel boasts a king, Solomon, whose wisdom is reputed to exceed that of the Egyptians. The Queen of Sheba, who is familiar with all Egypt has to offer, will decide the case for herself and spread the news, one way or the other, throughout the known world. Let us try to imagine for a moment this amazing scenario in its own time.

Traveling outside the cities could be dangerous in the ancient Near East. This general rule did not apply as readily to a royal caravan. Its sheer size would intimidate bandits as much as it impressed the peasants who watched the magnificent procession meander through the valley floor. From the garden roof of his palace, Solomon had watched royal caravans bring dignitaries to Jerusalem many times in the past. Like the others, this one was escorted by a modest but heavily equipped army, and accompanied by a lengthy chain of officials carried on lurching camels and, on foot, groups of attendants, scribes, musicians, cooks, and menial laborers. But this caravan was different because it carried within it none other than a leader who could influence world opinion, the Queen of Sheba, and she came to test Solomon. Based on her judgment, the tales about the wisdom of Solomon could be accredited in the international community as more than rumors; the surrounding nations would trust her ability to distinguish the kernel of Solomon's true sagacity from the husk of neighborly hearsay. All the surrounding nations would observe this event, obtaining from it a basis upon which to evaluate this king as well as the kingdom of Israel. And all this attention is suddenly focused on a king who was only the second in Jerusalem to have a palace of his own. So, we might imagine some of the excitement in the city on that day in the tenth century when Solomon watched from his palace roof the long, steady procession carrying the Queen of Sheba as it moved slowly up the road to the gates of Jerusalem.

The Queen of Sheba embodied all the polished diplomacy and elegance of a highly educated aristocracy. She could summon to her defense a wealth of wisdom traditions that had glittered as gold in the rich ore of Arabian culture for over a millennium. She appears to us as a worthy contender to Solomon in matters of wisdom, someone who would be familiar with the sapiential classics of the ancient Near Eastern world, especially those of Egypt. Scribes of lesser nations paid homage daily to the superior Egyptian traditions by transcribing them, and by imitating their style and content. King Solomon ruled a nation that had in his father's time been only a very fragile confederation of tribes. Israelites, as a nation, admitted their social inferiority to Egypt and to Egyptian wisdom every time they boasted of God's deliverance from slavery in that land. An admission of cultural inferiority to Egyptian wisdom could be said to belong to the words of Israel's national anthem.

But now Solomon's wisdom is allegedly greater than that of the Egyptians and all other leaders of nations in the Near East. So, the Queen of Sheba has packed her bags, summoned an entourage of servants, and traveled to Jerusalem with riddles which she would employ as part of her test of Solomon. Riddles provided a primary vehicle of testing in intellectual contests and competitions. If the reports the Queen of Sheba heard about Solomon prove to be true, he will be compared with the great geniuses of the day — e.g., Ethan the Ezrahite, and Heman, Calcol, and Darda, the sons of Mahol (1 Kgs. 4:31). If Solomon answers well, then Israel will be ranked among the wisest of nations — with Egypt, Edom, and Phoenicia. These thoughts would surely cross the agile mind of Solomon who waits for the Queen of Sheba to test him. The full account of Solomon's triumph on this occasion deserves our careful consideration:

And Solomon answered all her questions; there was nothing
hidden from the king which he could not explain to her. And
when the Queen of Sheba had seen all the wisdom of Solomon,
the house that he had built, the food of his table, the seating of
his officials, and the attendance of his servants, their clothing,
his cupbearers, and his burnt offerings which he offered at the
houseoftheLord,therewasnomorespiritin her (1Kgs.10:3-5).

She exclaims, "The report I heard was true ... I did not believe the
reports until I came and my own eyes had seen it ... your wisdom and
prosperity exceed the report which I had heard" (v. 6- 7). The queen
declares as "blessed" (cf. Psa. 1:1a; 2:11b) all those who serve
Solomon. She also blesses the God of Israel and the appointment of
Solomon as the king who will "execute justice and righteousness" (v.
9) in the land. After leaving gold, spices, and precious stones as gifts,
the queen returns to her land with a glowing report to make known
throughout the world.

This amazing story within the narratives about Solomon in 1
Kings is a realistic, history-like account, with sparse narrative
moments enriched by some marked attention to details, including
what the caravan carries, what the queen sees of Solomon's house,
and her florid response to his wisdom (vv. 6-9). Within this biblical
presentation of this event, the unnamed Queen of Sheba does not
seem to be merely a literary device nor is she merely a symbolic
figure, but she appears in the flesh and blood as a tough-minded
woman with her own *curriculum vitae*, well known then, though
totally unknown to us. This story, regarded by most historical critics
as a post-exilic legend, illustrates in miniature the transformation of
ancient Israelite wisdom to biblical wisdom and I will use it initially
as a focal point for my argument about the role of wisdom in the Old
Testament. Precisely because this scenario of the Queen of Sheba's
testing of Solomon belongs to the latest stages in the formation of the
Bible, it exhibits well various key features of wisdom in the context
of scripture, and especially in the Solomonic books of Proverbs,

Ecclesiastes, and Song of Songs. The key elements we will explore are (1) the relation between Israel's wisdom and that of Egypt, (2) a definition of wisdom by way of an analogy to the houses that Solomon has built, and (3) the question of what the riddles of the Queen of Sheba are and how Solomon should answer them. However, before we turn to these issues, we must review the current historical-critical circumstances that attend our investigation of wisdom in the context of scripture.

B. HISTORICAL CRITICISM AND ANCIENT ISRAELITE WISDOM

Rigorous historical examination has almost universally recognized the association of Solomon with the books of Proverbs, Ecclesiastes, and Song of Songs as a later imposition on earlier traditions. Form-critical studies recognize that Song of Songs is probably a collection of older erotic love songs. Though Solomon is mentioned at a few places, the book begins and concludes in the first person voice of a woman. Only the title links Solomon to the book as the author and its conformity to a fixed editorial formula is a sign that we cannot trust it historically. Ecclesiastes seems actually to have been assigned originally to someone else, "Qoheleth" — perhaps the title of an official, which Luther first translated as "the Preacher." It is true that other features now in the title and opening verses seem to identify Qoheleth with Solomon, but the reluctance to use the name "Solomon" confirms this effort as a secondary one. Likewise, the Hebrew of Ecclesiastes is obviously exilic or post-exilic, as indicated by the form of certain standard relative pronouns and other minor features. Finally, Proverbs offers little if any possibility of an origin with

Solomon. Prov. 25:1 contains a tantalizing historical note: "These are proverbs of Solomon which the men of Hezekiah king of Judah copied." This assertion of Solomon's authorship works ironically against the historical antiquity of these proverbs since it implies that Solomon's proverbs had neither been copied before nor were they well known for the two centuries between the time of Solomon and that of Hezekiah. Scribes apparently had to create a copy of "Solomonic" proverbs because a complete collection of Solomonic proverbs had not existed before. Scholars have also noted that the sayings in the book of Proverbs are limited to matters of general human conduct and morality, while the descriptions of Solomon's wisdom in 1 Kings stresses his skill in government (cf. 1 Kgs. 3:7-9, 3:16-28) and his encyclopedic knowledge of things such as flora and fauna (cf. 1 Kgs 4:33). Even William F. Albright, the dean of modern archaeologists who have questioned the excesses of historical criticism, concludes that the contribution of Solomon to Proverbs by the time of Hezekiah was probably "so archaic in content that they were no longer understood." Whatever older Solomonic core might have existed was supplemented by later sayings deemed to be worthy of Solomon's legendary wisdom.[1]

If these modern suspicions against the Solomonic derivation of the books of Proverbs, Ecclesiastes, and Song of Songs were not disappointing enough, R. B. Y. Scott wrote a brilliant, largely negative, traditio-historical essay in 1960 on the narrative about Solomon in 1 Kings 3-11. In brief, Scott demonstrated that these narratives were a composite of deuteronomistic traditions (seventh century or later) combined with some fragments of older tradition, as well as some later legends. He observed that the story of the Queen of Sheba's visit likely belongs to one of the latest levels in the redaction history of 1 and 2 Kings.[2] We can easily imagine its attraction for Jews in exile who yearned for national esteem and

---

1. William F. Albright, "Some Canaanite-Phoenician Sources of Hebrew Wisdom," *Supplements to Vetus Testamentum* 3 (1955), p. 13.

independence. Scott's contribution provides a seminal example of rigorous historical criticisim and our study will accept his conclusions as essentially valid.

The implications of these critical views are fully employed by James Crenshaw's standard textbook, *Old Testament Wisdom: An Introduction* (1981). Crenshaw, a leading wisdom scholar, thoroughly enjoys the iconoclastic implications of the recent historical investigations. After an overview of the story of the Queen of Sheba's visit, with an examination of its later interpretations, he observes, "An impregnable mountain called Fantasy stands between biblical interpreters and the historical Solomon."[3] Crenshaw punctuates his overview of the historical-critical evidence with blunt, pungent conclusions: "In short, Solomon's literary works either were non-existent or have disappeared"; and "In sum, our examination of the biblical traditions about Solomon's wisdom discovers no shred of evidence deriving from the era of that king."[4] Finally, he concludes, "Wisdom and Solomon have nothing to do with one another."[5] Crenshaw's strictly historical approach to wisdom presupposes a standard definition of wisdom in the ancient Near East, with its own distinct types of wisdom literature. He, then, evaluates the biblical traditions according to that standard. Employing this model of historical research we find little if any of the wisdom literature in the biblical books can be conclusively assigned to Solomon. Using this approach, scholars have widened the search to discover wisdom traditions and especially evidence of "wisdom influence" throughout the other books of the Bible as well.[6] The book

---

2. R. B. Y Scott, "Solomon and the Beginnings of Wisdom in Israel," *Supplements to Vetus Testamentum* 3 (1955) 262-79, reprinted in *Studies in Israelite Wisdom*, pp. 84-101, ed. James Crenshaw (New York: KTAV, 1976). See, also, R. B. Y. Scott, *The Way of Wisdom* (New York: The Macmillan Company, 1971), p. 95.

3. James Crenshaw, *Old Testament Wisdom: An Introduction* (Atlanta: John Knox Press, 1981), 44.

4. Crenshaw, *Wisdom*, pp. 48-49.

5. Crenshaw, *Wisdom*, p. 50.

of Job is consequently often treated as essentially a "wisdom" book while Song of Songs is frequently set outside of the provenance of wisdom entirely. The definition of wisdom in this approach is strictly based on an antiquarian estimate of what constituted wisdom in ancient times; its relation to the religious life of ancient Israel often becomes remote or wisdom is even set forward as an alternative to prophetic faith.[7] Conversely, only in the most recent period have we begun to appreciate once more how the canonical context of scripture provides warrants for discerning another, at times quite different, role for these traditions.

---

6.   R. B. Y. Scott, *The Way of Wisdom*, pp. 72-135 and Donn F. Morgan, *Wisdom in the Old
      Testament Traditions* (Atlanta: John Knox Press, 1981).

7.   Crenshaw, *Wisdom*, pp. 200-211, and Walter Brueggemann, *In Man We Trust: The Ne-
      glected Side of Biblical Faith* (Atlanta: John Knox Press, 1971), pp. 78-97.

C. SOLOMON AND SOLOMONIC WISDOM BOOKS AS SCRIPTURE

With the book of Psalms we observed how pre-biblical traditions *have become* scriptural only when they belong to a particular later context and intertext of scripture. This change in context also implies a change in the semantic import of these texts, now heard within a single tapestry of differing traditions woven together. Just as an old scrap of fabric may gain an entirely new purpose in the design of a quilt into which it is sewn, so a unit of tradition takes on a different semantic capacity when it is read and heard as scripture. Brevard Childs and Rolf Rendtorff have already shown in detail how Proverbs, Ecclesiastes, and Song of Songs have been editorially linked to the figure of Solomon. Consequently these traditions became, within the context of scripture, a collection of books definitive of biblical "wisdom," comparable to the association of Moses with the Torah and David with the Psalms.[8] This essay will presume that work is

8. Childs, *Introduction to the Old Testament*, pp. 545-59, 569-589, and Rendtorff, *The Old Testament*, pp. 255-57, 261-69.

readily available and will build upon it in some new directions. If we are going to come to terms with scripture, then we must take seriously the canonical context of scripture even though its realistic presentation may not always accord with our modern reconstructions of ancient history. Only after we have made this effort to comprehend the inner logic of scripture itself will we be in a position to ask critically how modern historical resources ought to be employed both to sustain and to illuminate such a text.

From a critical standpoint, the story of the Queen of Sheba becomes valuable precisely because it is a late addition, probably containing within its content a self-conscious awareness of a later scriptural understanding of wisdom that came to predominate within Judaism. From the standpoint of faith, we might conclude that editors of 1 and 2 Kings sought to discern through the Spirit of God how these traditions had the capacity to treasure Israel's historic testimony of God's revelation in history. In order to understand how scripture presented wisdom to Judaism in the post-exilic period and to later generations, we will take up the three aforementioned key elements in the story of the Queen of Sheba's visit to Solomon that convey some essential characteristics of biblical wisdom.

D. THE QUEEN OF SHEBA'S TEST

1. Israel's Wisdom and that of Egypt

The camaraderie that Solomon has with the Queen of Sheba and the implicit respect given to her ability conforms to a general picture in scripture of Israel's openness to the wisdom of other nations. At least within the canonical context of scripture, the editors responsible for the title of Psalm 72 want us to recall the episode in 1 Kings 10 as virtually an answer to prayer. The psalm asserts, "May gold of Sheba be given to him" (v. 15) and "May his name endure for ever, his fame continue as long as the sun. May men (here implicitly including women and even foreign men and women) bless themselves by him, (more so, may) all the nations call him blessed" (v. 17). This depiction of Solomon's desire for recognition by non-Israelite nations is complemented by evidence that Solomon borrows much of his wisdom from others. In the book of Proverbs, attributed to Solomon, we find the only places in the Bible where non-Israelite traditions are overtly adopted as Israelite tradition and authorial credit is even given to the foreign contributors (see the titles of 30:1; 31:1). Solomon is elsewhere portrayed as a collector of excellent proverbs wherever he can find them (Eccl. 12:9-10). Finally, thanks to modern archaeological discoveries and careful historical-critical investigation, we in the modern period can detect something that was perhaps taken for granted in the ancient period, namely, there are explicit allusions to parts of the internationally known Egyptian wisdom classic, The Teaching of Amen-em-opet, incorporated into Prov. 22:17-24:22.

Consider the implications of the dependence of biblical wisdom on foreign resources for the story of the Queen of Sheba's visit and in the canonical presentation in general. In the narrative of 1 Kings the testing of Solomon by the Queen of Sheba and his success precedes an unabashed celebration of his sagacity. The Queen of Sheba actually plays an authoritative role in confirming his wisdom. After this test and his brilliant adjudication of the disputed child of the two harlots (1 Kgs 3:10:16-28), Solomon's wisdom is compared to that of his Egyptian and other rivals in 1 Kgs. 4:30. Of course, the international status of Egypt as a center of wisdom is reported at various places in the OT (Gen. 41:8; Ex. 7:11; Isa. 19:11-15). This positive assessment of Egyptian wisdom, presupposed in the comparison of it with the wisdom of Solomon, stands in contrast to the negative portrayal of Egypt in other biblical traditions. Egypt elsewhere in scripture symbolizes the oppression from which the Hebrew slaves were rescued "with a mighty hand" (Dt. 9:26). Israel's prophets repeatedly warn Israel against the military alliances with other nations and reliance on their false prophets. The warnings in the book of Isaiah are exemplary, "Woe to those who go down to Egypt for help" (31:1). In other words, despite the warning of the prophets over and over about going down to Egypt and listening to their prophets, Solomonic wisdom seems to say, "What ever you do, be sure to obtain a library card at the University of Egypt and check out their best books!" This view of biblical wisdom implies that after you have read all of the Egyptian books, as well as those found in the smaller library of Jerusalem, you might become wise enough to be tested by some wisdom expert, like perhaps the Queen of Sheba. If she is sufficiently impressed, you could also make a lot of money in the process, with her serving almost as your patron and publicist.

At a minimum, this presentation of wisdom in scripture demonstrates that biblical wisdom bears a family resemblance to wisdom found elsewhere in the world. The depiction of Solomon's test conducted by the Queen of Sheba implies a situation in which he is vulnerable to the proverbs of the world even though the world may be ignorant of Israel's idiosyncratic language of faith. The conformity of biblical wisdom to this same standard of international wisdom explains why in the Solomonic books there occurs little or no reference to beliefs unique to Israel, including the giving of the law at Sinai, the memory of slavery in Egypt, the Exodus, the "covenant" with God or the "election" of Israel as a people chosen for a special historical purpose by Yahweh. This radical difference between the Solomonic books and other parts of scripture can be illustrated by observing how the Bible as a whole demands that we help the poor. Both the Torah and wisdom share justice and righteousness as common goals (cf. Prov. 1:3; 1 Kgs. 10:9). However, in the Torah the motivation for generosity to the poor and disadvantaged is frequently: "You will remember that you were once a slave in Egypt" (Dt. 15:15, 16:12). In Proverbs the same obligation to help the poor is found, but never because of a memory of slavery in Egypt. Instead, the motivation is broad enough to be relevant to every other nation: because to mock the poor is to insult God (17:5), or someday you may be in the same situation (21:13), or stealing from the poor will lead to your own poverty (22:16), or God will be their lawyer against you at the gate (22:22-23), or you will be cursed (28:27). In other words, these motivations found in biblical wisdom, as distinguished from the torah, conform to what international wisdom should understand. Israel's special language of faith is self-consciously bracketed out.

In the narrative about Solomon's receiving the gift of wisdom this same distinction is presupposed between a recognition of Solomon's wisdom and the additional requirement that he obey the law of God as David had done (1 Kgs. 3:14, 9:4-7). Behind this divine command is, once again, a recognition that wisdom and torah (including especially "law") are not identical. The possibility is established that one might be knowledgeable in wisdom but disobedient of the torah, or that one might be obedient to torah without being very wise in how that should be carried out. The nature of wisdom distinct from torah as depicted in the narratives of 1 Kings 3-10 corresponds to how the wisdom of the Solomonic books is distinct from the torah found elsewhere in scripture. In sum, scripture presents us with Solomonic wisdom as a territory of knowledge that self-consciously avoids the idiosyncratic language of Israelite faith found in the Torah of Moses and the Prophets in order to maximize the family resemblance between Israel's wisdom and that of other nations.

Despite these characteristics of biblical wisdom, it would be a mistake to assume from a modern perspective that scripture presents Solomon's wisdom as secular rather than religious, or as non-revelatory rather than divinely inspired. Wisdom, linked to the Solomonic books in the context of scripture, is clearly presented as an idiom of biblical revelation alongside the Torah of Moses (Genesis through Deuteronomy) and the Prophets. Solomon receives his wisdom in a vision as a gift from God. Wisdom in the context of scripture is not regarded as a secular pursuit or as knowledge gleaned solely from human experience. Some examples from the Solomonic books confirm this view. Prov. 2:6 affirms the divine origin of all wisdom as do the repeated assertions in Proverbs that wisdom begins in the "fear of the Lord" (cf. Prov. 1:7). The epilogue to Ecclesiastes editorially states the same (12:13- 14) and includes the Torah as a resource of Solomon's and Israel's wisdom (cf. Dt. 4:6). In a remarkable text in Prov. 30:1-6 we find a tough question raised by a foreigner, Agur son of Jakeh of Massa (uncertain): "I have not learned wisdom ... nor do I have knowledge of the Holy One. Who has ascended to heaven and come down ... What is his name, and what is his son's name? Surely you know!"(vv. 3-4). The answer is stated unequivocally, "The word of God proves true..." (v. 5a). This and the subsequent lines of the answer are actually citations from 2 Sam 22:31 and Dt. 4:2. By implication, the rest of scripture both ensures through divine revelation the possibility of human wisdom and provides an aide to the recognition of it, whether it is found in Israel or among the Egyptians.

2. The Houses that Solomon Builds and the House of Wisdom

In the account of the Queen of Sheba's visit, her evaluation of Solomon's wisdom entails more than a test with riddles. We may easily fail to notice the assertion that she is also convinced of his wisdom by what she sees: "the house that he built, the food of his table, the seating of the officials, and the attendance of his servants, their clothing, his cupbearers, and his burnt offerings which he offered at the house of the Lord" (1 Kgs. 10:4b-5a). Here the excellence of the houses Solomon has built, his personal household with all of its organization and his offering given at the temple (Hebrew uses here the same word "house") reflect the extent of his wisdom. This feature in the story points to one of the most consistent elements in the Bible's own internal definition of wisdom. The analogy of wisdom as the building and maintaining of a house, resembling that of the Egyptians or the other nations, proves to be a leading metaphor by which wisdom traditions came to be distinguished from both the torah and prophetic traditions within scripture.

The narrative about Solomon that surrounds the story of the Queen of Sheba's visit in 1 Kings 3-11 similarly confirms the relation of wisdom to the construction and maintenance of houses because it, too, depicts Solomon's wisdom as a gift that helps him build both his palace and the temple. A narrative framework has been most clearly established for all of the traditions about Solomon in 1 Kings by a series of editorial references to Solomon's relationship with the daughter of Pharaoh. Right at the beginning and, then, at the crucial turning points of the entire account, editorial notations about the daughter of Pharaoh occur (1 Kgs. 3:1, 7:8, 9:25, and 11:1). 1 Kings 3:1 introduces the entire narrative about Solomon with the assertion, "Solomon made a marriage alliance with Pharaoh's daughter, and brought her to the city of David, until he had finished building his own house and the house of the Lord and the wall around Jerusalem." The first episode following this introduction relates Solomon's receiving the gift of wisdom from God. Recall similarly in the Pentateuch that Bezalel and Oholiab are given "wisdom" (or "skill") from God to be artisans who construct the tabernacle (Ex. 31:1-6). The subsequent traditions in 1 Kgs. 5:1- 9:25 are editorially organized around the building activities. A series of editorial notes marks the completion of his own house (6:9, 14, 37; 7:1) and concludes with a reference to the daughter of Pharaoh: "Solomon also made a house like this hall for Pharoah's daughter whom he had taken in marriage" (7:8b). Next occurs a description of the building of the temple followed by a note confirming that it was completed (9:1), as were both houses (9:10). The narratives are even described in 9:15 as an "account of the forced labor which Solomon levied to build the house of the Lord and his own house...."

Once again, at the end of this entire account of house building, the editors recall the daughter of Pharaoh with whom this lengthy narrative began: "Pharaoh's daughter went up from the city of David to her own house which Solomon had built for her" (9:24). It is at this point that the visit of the Queen of Sheba occurs, with the celebration of Solomon's international reputation for wisdom. So far, Solomon has not been portrayed as disobedient to the torah of God, except for the brief comment in 3:3b. However, the next sequence of narratives categorically condemns him for breaking the law of God through idolatry, incited by his marriage to foreign wives, including "the daughter of Pharaoh" (11:1-2). In sum, editors have employed these references to the daughter of Pharaoh as a strategy to give coherence to these narratives and to assign Solomon's house building activities as well as the Queen of Sheba's test and the celebration of his wisdom to a period prior to his blatant disobedience of the torah which is recorded in 11:1.[9] Therefore, in the context of scripture, the core of these narratives about Solomon and the contents of Solomonic books are to be regarded as sources of wisdom complementary to torah obedience rather than, as was subsequently the case, endangered through torah disobedience. If wisdom teaches Israelites how to build a house as skillfully or better than the Egyptians, torah tells Israel how to act as a unique people of God in the world.

Besides the association of wisdom with the building of a house and all the organization and affairs of the household, we should note that the Queen of Sheba also observes as part of Solomon's wisdom his offering of sacrifices at the house of the Lord which he built. Consequently, the implicit definition of wisdom in this account includes the topics of "prayer" and "sacrifice" even though other peculiar aspects of religious faith, as we have seen, are bracketed out of the territory covered by biblical wisdom. This depiction of wisdom as pertaining to household matters, royal and domestic, as well as to matters of religious prayer and sacrifice accords remarkably well with the contents of the book of Proverbs. Similar to this story, the whole gamut of the common life, administration of households, the relation between neighbors, commerce, and inner-family relationships are a central concern. Also, despite the absence of key religious vocabulary found elsewhere in the Old Testament (the law, the Exodus, covenant, etc.), we do find several proverbs directly concerned with prayer and sacrifice (cf. Prov. 3:9; 15:8, 24; 17:1; 21:3, 27; 28:9). It seems that prayer, or aspects of what we

---

9. This redactional evidence is similarly assessed by Burke O. Long, *1 Kings: With an Introduction to Historical Literature* (Vol. IX in "The Forms of the Old Testament Literature" series; Grand Rapids: Eerdmanns, 1984), pp. 57-60, 113f.

often call today "spirituality," actually belongs to the international
vocabulary of wisdom whereas other religious subjects do not!

These observations lead us to consider more carefully the general
implications of the scriptural definition of wisdom as distinguished
from earlier wisdom traditions in Israel and the ancient Near East.
The matter is complicated by the probability that the historical
definition of wisdom probably changed over time and varied from
nation to nation. We confront this issue every time we try to decide
which ancient Near Eastern literature would be considered "wisdom
literature" in each specific country. For example, the Egyptian
school texts are more obviously labeled as wisdom than are the
Assyrian sources. Once the biblical context of wisdom is atomized
and the pre-biblical traditions are examined independently, the
problem of defining wisdom in ancient Israel proves to be a very
difficult one. Gerhard von Rad, for example, offered a compelling
possibility that wisdom, by gnomic and memorable expressions,
attempts to wrestle "order" out of the chaos of human "experience."[10]
Regardless of how attractive this general definition may be for
wisdom in ancient historical Israel, we should not fail to observe that
the scriptural presentation does not use either of these terms —
"order" or "experience" — even in traditions that seem in their
biblical pre-history to be the most obvious examples of wisdom,
originally and historically (e.g. much of Proverbs). Biblical wisdom
does not distinguish wisdom as non-revelatory as though ordinary
human experience were its basis in contrast to the Word of God.[11]

---

10. Gerhard von Rad, *Old Testament Theology*, trans. D. M. Stalker (New York: Harper & Row,
1962), p. 420, and his, "The Essentials for Coping with Reality," pp. 113-37, *Wisdom in Israel*,
trans. James D. Martin (New York: Abingdon Press, 1972).

11. See J. Coert Rylaarsdam, *Revelation in Jewish Wisdom Literature* (Chicago: University of
Chicago, 1946); Brevard S. Childs, "Revelation Through Wisdom," pp. 34-35, *Old Testament
Theology*; and H. Wheeler Robinson, "The Inspiration of the Sages," pp. 248-50, *Inspiration and
Revelation in the Old Testament* (Oxford: The Clarendon Press, 1946). On the relation of wisdom
to the religious cult, see Leo Purdue, *Wisdom and Cult*, (SBL DKS Series 50; Missoula: Scholar's
Press, 1977), pp. 135-260.

Furthermore, according to the prologue to Proverbs the ultimate goal of biblical wisdom is the same as the rest of the Old Testament, "righteousness, justice, and equity" (1:3), rather than a detached psychological or philosophical strategy to achieve "order" over "chaos." My thesis is that biblical wisdom came to be identified around a specific metaphor for wisdom and it is the term *house*, including house building and maintaining all the activities associated with a just, peaceful, and prosperous administration of a household.

An examination of Proverbs and Ecclesiastes demonstrates an overt editorial effort to relate wisdom in these books to the metaphor of a house. In Proverbs the most obvious indication of "house" as a metaphor for wisdom is found in the so-called personifications of wisdom in Prov. 9:1-2 which states: "Wisdom has built a house, she has slaughtered her beasts, she has mixed her wine, she has set her table." This assertion is surprising for several reasons. The statement that a woman builds a house occurs nowhere in scripture outside of Proverbs, nor in any other Near Eastern inscription. Based on what is known about houses in the ancient Near East, the idea of seven pillars instead of six seems strange and hard to imagine. The number may be chosen for numerological reasons as an expression of perfection. In any case, this striking image of wisdom as a woman building and arranging the affairs of a house has as its counterpoint the woman folly who has a house of her own (9:13-18) and who offers food and lodging to those who pass by. Similarly, the speech of the wanton woman in Prov. 7:10-27 contains an invitation to her house, where food, lavish furniture, fine linen, perfume, and sex are all offered as enticements; the account ends with a forboding observation, "her house is the way to Sheol, going down to the chambers of death" (v. 27, cf. 9:18).

This same metaphor of a house for wisdom and another for her rival, folly, is constitutive of individual proverbs as well. In Proverbs there is the so-called doctrine of the two ways, expressed by the polarity between wisdom and folly, righteousness and wickedness.

Elements in the latter pair can be found in Proverbs, though rarely elsewhere in scripture (cf. Mic. 6:10; Hab. 3:13), in the formulaic expression, "house of x." So, in Prov. 3:33 we find references to both the house of the righteous and the house of the wicked (also, cf. 12:7; 14:11; 15:6; 21:12), even as the same metaphor is applied to wisdom and folly in Proverbs 9. Furthermore, historical critics have generally accepted the idea that Proverbs 1-9 is an exilic introduction that includes older traditions composed at a time much later than the proverbial collections of Proverbs 10ff. If so, it is noteworthy that we most likely have in 14:1 and 24:3-4 editorial additions that highlight the metaphor of wisdom building a house. Prov. 14:1 states, "Wisdom builds her house but folly with her own hands tears it down"; while 24:3-4 declares, "By wisdom a house is built, and by understanding it is established, by knowledge the rooms are filled with all precious and pleasant riches." In redaction-critical terms, the editors responsible for the introduction to the book of Proverbs in chapters 1-9 have ensured that there occurs in what is now the second part of the book the same personification of wisdom constructing and caring for a household. Finally, the description of the ideal wife in the last chapter of Proverbs again illustrates wisdom in terms of all the related tasks of a household, including the production of commercial goods, the purchase of fields, raising children, food preparation, eloquent use of words, and the display of charm, beauty, and seduction (31:10-31).

An examination of Ecclesiastes for evidence of "house" used as a metaphor proves equally fruitful. From a redaction-critical perspective, the book seems to be a collection of aphorisms that are sometimes grouped topically together. The first of these begins with the words, "Vanity of vanity, says the Preacher, Vanity of vanities! All is vanity." These lines, or a shortened version of them occur at various places throughout the book though they are not the only repetition. What seems probable is that an editor at the last stages of the composition of the book added the same phrase after the last

124

aphorism in 12:8 and before the editorial epilogue in 12:9-14. The effect was to thematize the book as a whole and heighten the negative assessments found within it. The epilogue has clearly sought to guarantee that the book not be heard in isolation from the rest of scripture. A summary of wisdom has been offered reminding us that the Torah also remains a source of our wisdom (12:13). Moreover, it is significant that the prologue to the book explicitly identifies Qoheleth with Solomon by using the double device of calling him a "son of David, king in Jerusalem" and, then, by providing an assertion that he is one whose wisdom has never been surpassed (2:9; cf. 1 Kgs. 3:12).

What immediately contributes to our present concern are the autobiographical statements by Qoheleth-Solomon right at the beginning of the book of Ecclesiastes (2:1-8). There he asserts his desire to know both wisdom and folly. He describes this effort in terms of house building and related activities:

> I made great works; I built houses and planted vineyards for myself; I made myself gardens and parks, and planted in them all kinds of fruit trees. I made myself pools from which to water the forest of growing trees. I bought male and female slaves, and had slaves who were born in my house; I had also great possessions of herds and flocks, more than any who had been before me in Jerusalem. I also gathered for myself silver and gold and the treasure of kings and provinces; I got singers, both men and women, and many concubines, man's delight (v.v. 4-8).

This expression of a variety of things he does to explore wisdom corresponds well to what the Queen of Sheba sees as an indication of his wisdom in 1 Kgs 10:4-5, "the house that he had built, the food of his table, the seating of his officials, and the attendance of his servants, their clothing, his cupbearers, and his burnt offerings which he offered at the house of the Lord." Finally, when we examine the book of Ecclesiastes as a whole, a natural way to look for editorial influence other than at the beginning is, of course, at the end. There we find that the last aphorism (12:1-8a) is once again focused on the metaphor of a house, concluding with the editorial theme "Vanity of vanity":

> Remember also your Creator in the days of your youth, before the evil days come, and the years draw nigh, when you will say, "I have no pleasure in them," before the sun and the light and the moon and the stars are darkened and the clouds return after the rain; in the day when the keepers of the house tremble, and the strong men are bent, and the grinders cease because they are few, and those that look through the windows are dimmed, and the doors on the street are shut; when the sound of the grinding is low, and one rises up at the voice of a bird, and all the daughters of song are brought low; they are afraid also of what is high, and terrors are in the way; the almond tree blossoms, the grasshopper drags itself along and desire fails; because man goes to his eternal home, and the mourners go about the streets; before the silver cord is snapped, or the golden bowl is broken, or the pitcher is broken at the fountain, or the wheel broken at the cistern, and the dust returns to the earth as it was, and the spirit returns to God who gave it. Vanity of vanities, says the Preacher; all is vanity(12:1- 8).

What occurs here is, at a minimum, a confirmation of the theme of "vanity." No matter how wonderfully we construct a house and fill our lives with the benefits of wisdom, at death all our efforts languish and fade. If a young person should be encouraged to exploit the metaphor of wisdom in terms of building a new house, the elder sage by that same wisdom confronts in death the necessity of abandoning the house she or he has built, allowing it to fall into disrepair and ruin. The house that wisdom builds is always a temporary construction against the winds of time and the ravages of old age.

Finally, in Song of Songs, 8:6-7 stands out as an instance of editorial influence. It provides a proverb toward the end of the book that appears to summarize the significance of the entire Song. The most familiar lines in these verses remain, "Love is strong as death; (but) jealousy is cruel as the grave." A poetic depiction of the power of love concludes with the comment, "If a man offered for love all the wealth of his house, it would be utterly scorned." These words are cryptic, but they seem to convey the idea that love ought to have importance over everything else in one's house, or perhaps meta-phorically that love is at the top of the hierarchy of concerns within wisdom.

In sum, the biblical portrayal of wisdom carries its own inner-biblical definition, whether or not it corresponds with wisdom as practiced at different times in ancient Israel. A house and household is a subject of international interest maintained across the lines of religious differences. Part of the genuis of Jewish scripture is that it allowed for a profound discussion with the Egyptians and other nations on matters of wisdom without compromising the special religious language peculiar to Israel's understanding of the Torah and Prophets.

3. The Riddles of the Queen of Sheba

In the story about the Queen of Sheba in 1 Kings 10, she tests Solomon with "riddles." According to Andre Jolles, the great German interpreter of basic types of folklore, "Myth is an answer in which a question is presupposed; riddle is a question which provokes an answer."[12] Riddles are cleverly stated paradoxes that admit either

---

12. Andre Jolles, Einfache Formen: *Legende, Sage, Mythe, Rätsel, Spruch, Kasus, Memorabile, Märchen, Witz* (Tübingen: Max Niemeyer, 1974), p. 129. See, also, James Crenshaw, "Wisdom," pp. 225-64, in *Old Testament Form Criticism*, ed. John H. Hayes (San Antonio: Trinity Univeristy Press, 1974) and Roland E. Murphy, *Wisdom Literature: Job, Proverbs, Ruth, Canticles, Ecclesiastes, Esther* (Vol. XIII in "The Forms of the Old Testament Literature" series; Grand Rapids: Eerdmans, 1981).

to a single solution or perhaps to various solutions with differing degrees of satisfaction. If the common proverb explores a mystery or hidden truth based on an obvious analogy to our common experience, a riddle expresses a simple truth that will make no sense until the hidden analogy to our common experience can be found. Their usage could be playful and entertaining, ritualized and definitive of social status, as in this case of Solomon, or used as an ordeal to determine whether a prisoner should live or die. The only riddle preserved in the Bible can be found in Judg. 14:10-18. There a riddle is part of a contest at the wedding feast provided by Samson: "Out of the eater came something to eat; out of the strong came something sweet." The answer is "What is sweeter than honey? What is stronger than a lion?" Behind this response is an awareness of the possibility in nature that bees may form a honeycomb within the dried carcass of a dead lion. Behind this instance is the evidence that such riddles and riddle contests occur frequently in the stories we have from the ancient Near East. According to Prov. 1:6b, "riddles" are something to be mastered with the help of "proverbs." The numerical sayings in Prov. 6:16-19 and 30:15-31 may be designed especially for training sages in the art of answering riddles. In general, proverbs state in a simple way a cryptic truth about the world, while riddles express in cryptic form something that should be obvious, once we think carefully about it.

From within the logic of biblical realism, what specific areas of knowledge are covered by the riddles of the Queen of Sheba? Taking seriously the cumulative witness of scripture and its own idiomatic way of describing wisdom, we can, at the outset, focus on the metaphor of a house and the world of knowledge related to the care of a household. In order to understand this metaphor, we must also remember that in a pre-modern peasant economy the term "house" usually presupposes an extended family, almost a small village of its own. The house was a center of industry, a self-sufficient institution that contributed ideally out of its surplus of production to a religious administration and to a small group of ruling elders who channeled funds to community projects and festivals.[13] Once again we are helped by historical criticism not to substitute naively our modern view of a house for the conception of a house in the ancient Near East. Still, these related activities have much in common across international lines in spite of religious and historical differences. Regardless of our religious faith or economic status, whether we are kings, queens, or peasants, each of us tries to construct and maintain a dwelling place for ourselves and our families. We prepare meals, raise families, run the household industries, tend the gardens, direct those who serve, have sex, enjoy good music, entertain, teach, repair and invent implements for our work, adjudicate disputes, and we pray and offer sacrifices. Even today we express such wisdom in the form of proverbs and especially riddles; modern advertising has effectively capitalized on the conciseness of wisdom sayings and their traditional promises of happiness, success, and health.

In the biblical presentation riddles often cover areas associated with our modern conceptions of science and psychology in which simple and elegant explanations are drawn from the observation of complex or enigmatic data. This scientific dimension in the riddles of wisdom is expressed in the psychological and socially analytic character of many proverbs and aphorisms in the Solomonic books and by a description of the natural world as part of the territory embraced by Solomon's wisdom: "He spoke of trees, from the cedar that is in Lebanon to the hyssop that grows out of the wall; and he spoke also of beasts, and of birds, and of reptiles, and of fish" (1 Kgs. 4:33). In sum, biblical proverbs and riddles complement each other by presenting us in the modern period with antique epistemological strategies that strive to comprehend the world that God has created and revealed to us as well as the nature of life together within it. This

---

13. E. R. Wolf, *Peasants* (Englewood Cliffs: Prentice-Hall, 1966) and Norman Gottwald, *The Hebrew Bible: A Socio-Literary Introduction* (Philadelphia: Fortress Press, 1985), pp. 321-25.

large implicit arena of "wisdom" within scripture, so circumscribed by the context of Solomonic traditions and distinguished from torah and prophecy, influenced directly how pre-modern Jewish and Christian interpreters read the scripture as an authority in matters of faith and conduct. As just one example, as late as the seventeenth century Anglican Bishop Joseph Hall could title his topical organization of citations from the three Solomonic books: *Salomons Divine Arts, of 1. Ethickes, 2. Politickes, 3. Oeconomicks: That is, the Government of 1. Behaviour, 2. Commonwealth, 3. Familie* (1609).

With this recognition of how the Old Testament has presented wisdom as an idiom of revelation, I want to consider some aspects of wisdom literature within Christian scripture as a whole that are especially relevant to the current debate over the authoritative use of scripture: Topics treated more in wisdom than in other parts of the Bible, and the role of wisdom hermeneutically to inform how scripture is read as an authority in matters of faith and conduct.

E. SPECIAL TOPICS OF WISDOM

Old Testament wisdom often treats subjects unaddressed in the Torah and the Prophets, and even missing in the Christian New Testament traditions, regardless of whether they are wisdom in character (e.g., James) or not. For example, outside of the Old Testament wisdom literature, the subject of human sexual conduct in the Bible is primarily addressed in terms of prohibition and taboo. The Torah condemns certain behaviour without offering much affirmation of sexual pleasure or eroticism even in marriage. The prophets call attention to sexual abuse without celebrating the ecstasy of human love. The strongest affirmation of human sexuality might be found indirectly in the way the book of Hosea has taken up the language of erotic love and translated the vocabulary of sin and transgression into it. So, rebellion against God becomes identified with harlotry (Hos. 1:2; 4:12,15; 5:4) and transgression of God's command is cast in the language of marriage infidelity (Hos. 5:7; 7:4). In spite of the largely pejorative use of sexual language, the passion and eros of Hosea in his determination to win back Gomer's loyalty is made analogous to God's equally passionate, irrational, and unrelenting love for Israel that will not let go of the elect even though God's overtures have been repeatedly spurned. The New Testament offers little by way of a corrective to this backhanded affirmation of sexuality. Brevard Childs concisely summarizes the New Testament witness:

> Of course, the New Testament does contain explicit impera-
> tives instructing husbands to love their wives (Eph. 5:5; Col.
> 3:19), but still this does not offset the general tendency of the
> New Testament to assign sexual passion to the category of hea-
> then immorality, or at least to regard it as a danger to be
> extinguished (1 Cor. 7:9). [14]

My point is that sexuality is one of those subjects within Christian scripture that finds its positive formulation more in Old Testament wisdom texts than in the Torah, the Prophets, or even the Gospels and the Pauline Epistles. The closest counterparts to Old Testament wisdom in the New Testament include some of the teachings of Jesus, some of Paul's instruction (cf. 1 Corinthians 13), including the Pauline advice to various members of the household in the pastorals, as well as the book of James. These New Testament resources, in my view, pale by comparison with the treatment in the Solomonic wisdom literature of sexuality and eroticism, especially the Song of Songs. Since the New Testament presupposes the Old Testament as part of Christian scripture, the church that *does not* preach from the Old Testament implicitly takes a Marcionite position. Moreover, the church that *cannot* preach from the Old Testament wisdom literature will be doomed to an impoverished scriptural understanding of love, sensuality, and eroticism. What is true of human sexuality and the Old Testament wisdom literature pertains as well to many other areas of Christian conduct and knowledge, including insight from psychology, the social sciences, and an

---

14. Brevard S. Childs, "Proverbs, Chapter 7, and A Biblical Approach to Sex," p. 199, in his *Biblical Theology in Crisis.*

encyclopedic or scientific knowledge of the world.[15]

1. Wisdom as a Hermeneutical Guide

Another primary role for biblical wisdom within Christian scripture is the help it gives to biblical interpreters who, by the mastering of riddles shared with the world, can frame more precisely the questions that are, then, brought to the Torah, the Prophets, and the Gospel. Though the human witness of the scripture remains the same over time, each new generation brings to it a different acuity regarding God's revelation of reality and how that vision of reality might be illuminated by the Bible's subject matter, the Gospel of Jesus Christ. Historical criticism belongs to this wisdom which is essential for our precise understanding of the grammar and etymology of the biblical text and which ought to give greater, rather than less, acuity to our pragmatic vision of the scripture as a literal witness to divine revelation. Wisdom, also, throws into suspicion the questions we bring to that perception of the scriptural text so that we might alter, refract, or refine how we form our questions. We should not be surprised that foolish questions often fail to find profound answers in biblical interpretation. This very principle explains why we read scripture again and again, trusting that with maturity and new knowledge of God's revelation of the world the sophistication of our own riddles will increase so that we might hear a new word from God to which we were not receptive before. Hence, wisdom ought to refine the quality of the role played by the two major agents within the so-called "hermeneutical circle," that is to say, the role played both by the scripture text itself and by the reader.

Related to this role of wisdom is an awareness that wisdom, as distinct from folly, ought to expose the prejudice and self-interest of

---

15. For an overview on wisdom in Christian scripture, see G. T. Sheppard, "Wisdom," pp. 1074-82, in *The International Standard Bible Encyclopedia*, ed. G. W. Bromiley (Grand Rapids: Eerdmans, 1988), Vol. 4; and *Aspects of Wisdom in Judaism and Early Christianity*, ed. Robert L. Wilken (Notre Dame: University of Notre Dame Press, 1975).

both the human witness of scripture and that of the reader. In its human form the witness of the biblical text can be shown by the wisdom of historical criticism to be riddled with its own cultural myopia, social prejudice, sexism, homophobia, racism, nationalism, and foolish assumptions about the world. This human witness of scripture is interpreted by modern readers who can be shown by a similar wisdom to be equally subject to cultural myopia, social prejudice, sexism, racism, homophobia, nationalism, and foolish assumptions about the world. Nonetheless, these readers interpret scripture in hope for a Word of God that puts under judgement everything culturally myopic, socially prejudiced, sexist, racist, homophobic, or distorted by foolish assumptions about the world. Precisely because Christians have faith that such an understanding of scripture is possible, they can bring expectations informed by wisdom that predispose their generation to learn some new things about the Gospel that others may have failed to realize before. So, for example, a new understanding of the implications of the equality of men and women can be shown to be at the center of the Gospel in a way that both challenges current church policies and causes us to notice as never before the patriarchalism inherent in the human nature of the biblical testimony itself. The limitations of both may be thrown into sharper relief by the light of the Gospel. These limitations are overcome by the way in which scripture is read, according to its context or scope, in association with its subject matter, and in the discernment of the Holy Spirit. For this reason, Flacius in the sixteenth century could affirm the inerrancy of scripture while acknowledging that a proper reading of the Bible finds there some elements that are "alien" and "false" in terms of that subject matter. His advice is that we should memorize such texts and pray about them in hope that we might find their literal sense.[16] Not every text offers the same clarity in terms of its role as witness to God's

16. Flaccius, *De Ratione*, p. 93.

revelation. What should be clear is that the final goal of interpreting the Bible biblically ought not to be an encounter with the Bible as literature, but an encounter with the Word of God which is the same as the Gospel of Jesus Christ.

2. Wisdom and the Politics of Slavery, Women's Ordination, Gender and Sexuality

The aim of this book has been to present an alternative to the polarity of liberalism and literalism in the current debate over how to interpret the Bible. This purpose has precluded any detailed consideration of specific contemporary issues and how the Bible best contributes to theological arguments about them. David Kelsey's *The Uses of Scripture in Recent Theology* (1975) has already demonstrated various problems that must be confronted whenever we seek to adjudicate different authoritative appeals to scripture.[17] Theological arguments inherit the same problems as do any philosophical defenses of truth, though theology may volunteer at the outset the necessity of some faith and the language of faith from which reason begins to seek understanding, from faith to faith. Within the limits of this present study, only a few observations can be offered here regarding how the context of scripture might affect arguments for biblical revelation about the nature of reality and, more practically, our life together. These observations will consist of a few comments on each of three topics: slavery, women's ordination and issues of gender, and sexuality.

a. Slavery

The question of how Christians should respond to slavery deserves our attention today even though it is no longer a contemporary

---

17. David Kelsey, *The Uses of Scripture in Recent Theology* (Philadelphia: Fortress Press, 1975), pp. 122-55.

controversy. Almost every Christian considers the matter settled and has confidence that the Gospel condemns slavery as an institution. Of course, in the early to mid-1800's, there was a bitter debate in the United States on this subject. Denominations split, a Civil War was fought, and the biblical and theological scholars provided copious arguments pro and con. Charles Hodge, a theologian at Princeton Seminary, concluded that the Bible condones slavery by saying, "If the present course of abolitionists is right, then the course of Christ and the apostles were (sic!) wrong. For the circumstances of the two cases are ... in all essential particulars, the same." The renowned biblical scholar, Moses Stuart, at Andover Newton could conclude only that the Bible gave mixed signals.[18]

Without reviewing all of the relevant biblical texts, it is important to note that the Bible never explicitly condemns slavery and Jesus is silent on the subject. Conversely, the topic of slavery is considered in numerous laws in the Mosaic Torah in a manner that seem to accept the institution of slavery and set limits to brutality, requiring recompense according to the nature of the injury to slaves. While the New Testament book of Philemon might imply a change in the relationship between master and slave, Paul does not explicitly demand freedom for Onesimus. In the pastoral epistles within the collection of the Pauline books, 1 Tim. 6:1-5 bluntly and clearly dissuades any slave from demanding freedom from his or her Christian owner.

Against a reading of these texts as a rationale in support of contemporary forms of slavery, one could argue from a hearing of the Gospel itself within the canonical context of scripture as a whole. Statements about the Gospel throughout scripture and the hope it engenders regarding the nature of human existence agree that all people are made in the image of God so that slavery can never be

---

18. This information is taken from Willard Swartley's *Slavery, Sabbath, War, and Women: Case Issues in Biblical Interpretation* (Kitchener: Herald Press, 1983), pp. 37, 54.

grounded on a theory of racial inferiority. The Prophets and the Gospels depict a demand for justice that breaks with cultural and racial barriers. The apocalyptic hope of these materials point in a direction that would undo any legalistic subordination of one person to another. As discussed in chapter one, even the laws in the Torah are presented as two different sets of laws, one given to Moses at Sinai and another version in Deuteronomy where Moses "interprets" or "explains" (Dt. 1:5) the revealed law to the next generation about to enter the Promised Land. Therefore, biblical law, including the legislation from Sinai does not have a fixed expression but requires interpretation according to the wisdom of God and the circumstances of a later generation. This wisdom, aided by historical criticism, shows that slavery had its own social function in the ancient period different than later forms of it, although we may still believe that even in the past it was unjustified.

This lack of correspondence to contemporary forms of slavery is undermined even more by a growing awareness that the harm done far outweighs any pretense of benefit to those who were kidnapped from their native land. If slavery under the circumstances described in the Bible might have been able to survive alongside the Torah and the Gospel, at least the slavery that we have come to know could not and that awareness properly warrants our modern suspicions about any rationalization for slavery of any sort, even in ancient times. Finally, we can argue from the depictive realism of the biblical accounts that Israel's slavery in Egypt corresponds to and illuminates the circumstances of slavery in the United States. Slaves began to see themselves rendered as figures in the universal reality as depicted in scripture so that they learned in scripture how to lament in prayer and to seek the hand of God through the actions of ordinary people in the struggle for freedom.[19] There is no simple prooftext available for this argument because the norm for our decision must

19. James Cone, "Biblical Revelation and Social Existence," pp. 62-83, *God of the Oppressed* (New York: Harper & Row, 1975), pp. 62-83.

be not the actual words of any particular biblical text but the subject matter of scripture itself, the Gospel of Jesus Christ: the Way, the Truth, and the Life.

The possibility that we can receive new insight into God's revelation is ensured only by the Holy Spirit but we can prepare ourselves for it by the exercise of Solomonic wisdom, including a socio-literary-historical awareness of the tensions in the biblical witness on this matter of slavery and an equally serious historical, economic, political, ethical, and social psychological investigation of contemporary slavery. Without as much wisdom as possible, we either fail to hear scripture in its own human terms or we bring to our interpretation only a prejudicial knowledge of slavery based on our own folly. In the exercise of this wisdom we learn from scholars, journalists, articulate slaves, and people of extraordinary knowledge wherever they may be found.

Finally, the canonical context of scripture orients our hearing of the human witness in terms of its subject matter. Wisdom ought to give to our perception of the tensions within the scriptural witness a new precision that resists every temptation to harmonize away the differences. We are induced by the context of scripture itself to discern both how the Gospel is the object of this biblical witness and how the Gospel sheds light on the particular issue of contemporary slavery. In this way, biblical revelation is neither reduced to secular wisdom nor is the nature of the Gospel divorced from it. Though the actual words of the scripture do not change, our capacity to hear the Gospel as their subject matter may be enhanced so that we gain a fresh and perhaps radically different grasp of what the Gospel requires of us from that of our predecessors within the same Christian tradition. We are still mired in many of our own prejudices, but this one we have, thank God, finally "seen" to be under divine judgment. Consequently, anyone today who seeks to justify slavery and racial prejudice by scripture must do so with a foolishness more culpable than that of earlier generations of Christian interpreters. The Church

138

in this sense does not seek to go back to the Bible without moving, at the same time, forward to the Gospel.

b. Women's Ordination and Issues of Gender

The role of wisdom in the theological interpretation of scripture in these matters is comparable at points to that we have seen in the debate over slavery. In this section I want to examine three illustrations, starting with the issue of women's ordination. When the General Council of the United Church debated the ordination of women in 1926, the report published the following year illustrates how remarkably the dictates of wisdom have changed from then to now. The overview of the biblical evidence of women in leadership roles and especially the estimate of the role women played in the early centuries of the church has become severely out-dated by recent scholarship. The church report attempted to define an office of the diaconate as a category of women's ministry distinct from another predominately male "ordered" ministry. The use of the Bible in their effort to find an historical precedence for this division of ministry between men and women now appears naive and pre-critical.

The report assigned the ordination of women to the diaconate on grounds that married women could not devote themselves to the ministry as a "primary and life-long vocation." The crude expression of this prejudice appears in the minority report which warns of "the not very edifying spectacle of the husband keeping house while the wife is engaged in public duties." [20]

This modern pejorative view of "married" women in the ordered ministry was reflected once again in the church deliberations of the early 1960's. Again, the reports on the Old and New Testament and roles of women in church history are obviously quite dated, since they occur prior to a wealth of new studies on these subjects in the

20. "Report on the Committee on the Ordination of Women" (United Church, 1927), p. 14.

1970's and 80's.[21] It is too far too easy for us to become self-righteous when we see the prejudice of the past. As with the issue of slavery in the 1840's and 50's, a later wisdom makes some of the older arguments seem preposterous in retrospect. Such is the nature of wisdom that each generation can feel superior to the past while nurturing its own repressed prejudice with comparable folly. Despite this irony in our pursuit of truth and justice, the way we hear scriptures does change according to our new understanding of both the biblical witness itself and the socio-political history of prejudice against women. Wisdom implies that in time we should attain new insight and, therefore, ask questions of the Gospel in a different way, and hopefully with a new precision, than did earlier generations. After all, "the Gospel" is not the name of a place at which we arrive, it is a path, a "Way," that leads us in faith, as it did preceding generations, toward the full Truth of God revealed in Christ Jesus.

A second observation about the role of wisdom concerns its assessment of the biblical text itself. Wisdom provides one of the primary biblical idioms by which we seek to evaluate the literal sense of scripture, including its circumstantial limitations, as a witness to the Gospel. On this subject, I want to call attention to one feature of the Geneva New Testament of 1602. The Geneva Bible preceded the King James version and dominated as the preachers' Bible for about a century. Its marginal notes came from Theodore Beza, the continental protege of John Calvin, with some expansions by the English protestants who cherished it from about 1560 to the 1640's. On 1 Corinthians 11, the marginal notes stress the subordination of women but also try to assert some ideal sense of "mutual conjunction" in their roles respective to men. For our purpose, a verse I had not often noticed received unique attention, including an italicized marginal note. Verse four reads in the Geneva: "Every

---

21. See the report of the Commission on Ordination, pp. 370-99, in the "Record of Proceedings" (United Church, 1962).

man praying or prophecying having any thing on his head, dis-
honoureth his head." The problem with this verse was that in the
seventeenth century, every man with any self-esteem wore a hat
when he prayed in public or preached. The marginal note states, "It
appeareth, that this was a politike lawe serving only for the circumstances of the time that Paul lived in, by this reason, because in these
our dayes for a man to speake bare headed in an assembly, is a signe
of subjection." [22]

Therefore, even the protestant "restorers of the Gospel" used the
logic of wisdom to recognize the circumstantial quality of the
biblical witness so that the actual words of a text would not be treated
uncritically as identical with the eternal truth of the Gospel any more
than should the particular verbal expression of a single biblical law,
including even one of the Ten Commandments. [23] By appeal to the
canonical context of each biblical text, the Reformers sought to find
clues regarding the circumstantial nature of the biblical witness and
how it could be heard critically as a testimony to God's revelation.

Another concern related to the use of wisdom is the contemporary debate over "inclusive language." From the standpoint of
biblical wisdom the witness of scripture ought never to be absolu-
tized in its language so that it is uncritically confused with the
language of faith. The Christian church has periodically in its history
condemned as anathema the assumption that God is "masculine."
The predominant masculine imagery about God helps to secure the
"personal" nature of God, but even earlier generations knew in their
best theological wisdom that God is not "a man," in any gender-
related analogical sense. It is true that the personal nature of God

22. *The Geneva New Testament: The Annotated New Testament, 1602 Edition: With Introductory
Essays*, ed. G. T. Sheppard (New York: Pilgrim Press, 1989), p. 85.

23. Cf. Karl Barth, "The Reality of the Divine Command," pp. 63- 115, in his *Ethics*, trans. G. W.
Bromiley (New York: Seabury Press, 1981): "Moral generalities of any kind, even though they
be biblical and in the exact words of the Bible, are not the command, for over against them we
ourselves secretly are and remain judges and masters. The good is this or that command that is
given to me without choice or determination on my part" (p. 83).

could have been expressed more frequently in scripture by female imagery, so that the predominance of male imagery does exert an undue connotative influence upon the reader. This aspect of the biblical witness is exacerbated by many other patriarchialistic features, including the predominant presentation of Old Testament prophets as male and the emphasis on males within the Twelve in the depiction of Jesus' ministry. Both of these impressions given by the biblical text can be questioned on historical-critical grounds.

As an historical critic, I agree with scholars, such as Elizabeth Fiorenza, that the editors of scripture betray an inordinant disposition to give credit to male figures and to support their own prejudice in various other ways in which scripture has taken its present shape.[24] Nevertheless, I would reject any assumption that we can recover a better norm of God's revelation by substituting for the witness of scripture a reconstruction of ideal egalitarian moments in the history of either Israel or the first followers of Jesus. While such moments may, in fact, better model the hope of the Gospel than some aspects of the biblical witness itself, one cannot properly be substituted for the other without misunderstanding a basic conception of the sufficiency of scripture. The scripture, despite the poverty and limitations of its witness, still succeeds in conveying a knowledge of the Gospel, a Gospel that puts both the interpreter and the human witness of scripture under judgment.

An irony exists in that the Gospel we come to know through

---

24. Cf. Elizabeth Schüssler Fiorenza, *In Memory of Her: A Feminist Theological Reconstruction of Christian Origins* (New York: Crossroad, 1986), pp. 48-56. The recent literature is extensive, including, for example, Mieke Bal, *Murder and Difference: Gender, Genre, and Scholarship on Sisera's Death* (Bloomington: Indiana University, 1988): Phyllis Bird, "Images of Women in the Old Testament," pp. 41-88, in *Religion and Sexism*, ed. Rosemary R. Ruether (New York: Simon and Schuster, 1974) and her "Translating Sexist Language as a Theological and Cultural Problem," *USQR* 42 (1988) 89-95: *Feminist Perspective on Biblical Studies*, ed. A. Y. Collins (Chico: Scholars Press, 1985); *Gender and Difference in Ancient Israel*, ed. Peggy Day (Minnesota: Fortress Press, 1989); and Phyllis Trible, *Texts of Terror: Literary Feminist Readings of Biblical Narrative* (Philadelphia: Fortress Press, 1984).

scripture regarding the equality of women and men increases the very wisdom by which we are able to detect patriarchalisms inherent in the human witness of scripture itself. The biblical witness becomes, because of the Gospel, more rather than less offensive in its human form. This difference between the sufficient capacity of scripture to bear witness to its subject matter and the distance that subject matter engenders between itself and the limits of its human witness accounts for the necessity of interpretation and preaching. While the Bible itself often fails to use inclusive language, a minister of the Gospel on the basis of that witness should know better. It is one thing to empathize with the logic of past generations so that we do not become hopelessly self-righteous, it is another to perpetuate the prejudice of the past on the false grounds of preserving the truth of a tradition.

c. Sexuality

As mentioned before, wisdom literature plays a particularly important role in the biblical presentation of eroticism and sexuality. An examination of the politics of sexuality within the biblical wisdom books prepares us to answer the riddles of the Queen of Sheba on this subject in certain specific ways. First, the eroticism of the Egyptians or the Sabeans participates in a similar sapiential logic as that of Israel, of later Jews and Christians. A number of riddles about sexuality derive from the biblical recognition that the language of seduction by which the wanton woman lures the foolish passerby in Proverbs 7 is the same language that articulates a subject of joy and ineffable pleasure in the Song of Songs.[25] The same eroticism implicit in the appeal of Woman Folly in Prov. 9 occurs again in the appeals of Woman Wisdom to those who would learn to be sages and advocates of justice and righteousness. The same rhetoric and language of seduction entice potential students to take opposing

25. Childs, "Proverbs," *Biblical Theology in Crisis,* pp. 186-190.

143

paths, one leading to personal fulfillment, pleasure, success, peace, and health, while the other leads to self-destruction and "the chambers of death" (Prov. 7:27). Though the words of love may sound the same, the consequences can be antithetical.

Another implication of biblical wisdom for human sexuality is that eroticism is never portrayed as a bridge to the divine. Moreover, the logic and politics of sexuality does not need to import into its proverbs pious talk drawn from elsewhere in scripture. In a wisdom discussion of sex, Jews and Christians often express their knowledge in ways that resemble the riddles and proverbs of non-believers. The Song of Songs illustrates this dimension in so far as it does not even indicate clearly whether the lovers whose erotic love it celebrates are married. The subjects of marriage and monogamy are certainly important ones for Christian, but they cannot be treated adequately within scripture from the logic of wisdom alone. Nevertheless, sexuality would appear to be one subject about which Jews and Christians should invite the Queen of Sheba to come and test them. In other words, unless Christians are prepared to answer the riddles of the sexologists, they are not on biblical grounds ready either to cite properly or to understand fully the true implications of torah, prophecy, or gospel on such matters.

Solomon is portrayed in scripture as someone who masters the wisdom in the world but finally refuses to obey the teaching of the Torah. The narratives about Solomon do, however, contain a warning that is repeated in various ways throughout scripture. After Solomon had completed building the houses and before the visit of the Queen of Sheba he offers a lengthy dedication for the house of the Lord and a prayer to God (1 Kings 8:22-61). God, then, appears to him "a second time as he had appeared to him at Gibeon" (9:1; the first time he received the gift of wisdom), with a demand once again that he must also obey the law, "my commandments and my statues" (v. 6). If Solomon does not, God warns, "this house will become a heap of ruins" (v. 8) and, accordingly, Israel will become a "a proverb and a byword" among the nations. Even if Solomon answers all the riddles of the Queen of Sheba, he must also pass God's test of obedience to the revealed law. So, there is in the scriptural presentation of wisdom a tension between mastering riddles of all the other nations, on the one hand, and remaining obedient to the peculiar revelation of the law and the prophets, on the other. These observations suggest that as Jews and Christians we are not to be satisfied with the sapiential consequences of our actions, but, also, must consider whether our actions violate peculiar norms of love and justice revealed by the other parts of scripture. Yet, the aim of Christianity is not to articulate and to defend a particular fixed "morality" in the world, which the Gospel itself puts under judgment. Even so, Christians are not lost in a moral wasteland of ambiguity, but find in Jesus Christ a sure sense of direction toward the way, the truth, and the life. Words about fidelity, covenant, and commitment are, therefore, basic to the vocabulary of a Christian understanding of love and justice.

The subject of homosexuality illustrates how our understanding of wisdom, especially how we have begun to answer the riddles of sexology in the last few decades, has radically changed how we formulate and direct questions to scripture for normative guidance. Only in the recent period has it become the case that so many Christians, including conservative evangelicals, have concluded that most homosexual persons have something we call a "sexual orientation." Also, most church pronouncements now conclude that one's sexual orientation is not usually a matter of choice but is determined either by genetic or a psycho-social fixation in early childhood. Efforts to change a person's sexual orientation have been largely accepted as futile. For that reason, a typical conservative evangelical position now allows that a Christian may be same-sex oriented and accepted as a member of the church, though he or she must refrain from any erotic consummation. One biblical problem with that position is the realization that "sex and celibacy ... is a polarity totally

foreign to the Old Testament."[26] The New Testament admonitions,
in my view, against marriage as a distraction in view of the impend-
ing return of Christ, have equally little to do with a later church notion
of celibacy. In other words, the wisdom literature of the Bible challenges us to refine our questions so that the response of the Gospel
to them will possibly be different from that of earlier generations. In
my view, neither the revealed Torah nor the Gospel precludes the
modern possibility of covenanted partnerships between persons of
the same sexual orientation. These relationships would be similar to
marriages, in which the faithful love for one another is analogous to
that mystery of God's unrelenting love for each of us, in spite of all
our human failings. [27]

At a minimum, biblical wisdom serves as a warning to any
church which can barely talk about issues of masturbation and
eroticism in monogamous marriages, that it should be cautious about
how boldly it judges the loving sexuality of same-sex oriented
Christian sisters and brothers. Solomon ultimately failed because,
despite his wisdom, he did not seek to know and to obey the Torah;
conversely, there is the danger today that Christians may claim to
know the demands of the Law and the Gospel without nurturing
wisdom in the very areas of human life they most wish to influence.

26. Ibid., p. 190.

27. The recent literature has become extensive, including: John Boswell, *Christianity, Social
Tolerance, and Homosexuality: Gay People in Western Europe from the Beginning of the
Christian Era to the Fourteenth Century* (Chicago: University of Chicago 1980); Peter Brown,
The Body and Society: Men, Women, and Sexual Renunciation in Early Christianity (New York:
Columbia University, 1988; and Robin Scroggs, *The New Testament and Homosexuality*
(Philadelphia: Fortress Press, 1983). From a conservative evangelical perspective, see, for
example, Letha Scanzoni and Birginia Mollenkott, *Is the Homosexual My Neighbour*? (San
Francisco: Harper & Row, 1978) and the books and articles reviewed in the "Record," the
newsletter of a nation-wide organization called "Evangelicals Concerned": c/o Dr. Ralph Blair,
311 E. 72nd St., New York, NY 10021. For a more detailed argument on these subjects by the
author, see G.T. Sheppard, "The Use of Scripture within the Christian Ethical Debate Concerning
Same-Sex Oriented Persons," *Union Seminary Quarterly Review* 40/1&2 (1985) 13-36 and
"Human Sexuality and Biblical Revelation," pp. 233-47, in *AIDS Issues,* ed. David Hallman (New
York: Pilgrim Press, 1989).

The Bible in one hand and foolishness in the other can do as much violence to the aims of divine justice as did Solomon's disobedience of the Torah despite his renowned wisdom.

Finally, I want to conclude this investigation of biblical wisdom, which has focused especially on the Old Testament, by affirming that the present hope of the church lies, in my view, neither in the older liberal nor so-called "literalist" or conservative-fundamentalist positions. My own position has sought to find in the canonical context of scripture itself and in the church's tradition of biblical interpretation resources for a confessional stance, one that affirms the significance of God's revelation as the basis of Christian faith. Wisdom, as I have tried to show, belongs to scripture not as a secular alternative but as one of the idioms of biblical revelation. My approach is neither to advocate a natural theology nor to deny that God's revelation manifests itself in limited forms to all people. Biblical wisdom challenges both Jews and Christians to have a conversation with the world, without denying special revelation unique to the hope of each faith. In the New Testament, Jesus Christ fulfills the promise of the Old Testament, appearing to us as one who is both a prophet "more glorious" than Moses (Heb. 3:1-6) and a wisdom teacher greater than Solomon (Matt.12:42; Lk. 12:27). As Christians we should accept the full scandal of our faith, while acknowledging the independent worth of Jewish scripture, on the one hand, and while seeking to rival the world in proverbs and riddles true to the wisdom of God on the other.